Language, Translation and Management Knowledge

The book provides insights, description and analysis over the knowledge production process within business, organization and management research. Importantly, it does so from a language and translation perspective. It critically engages with the role of English in this process and provides theoretical argument for the need to include multilingualism in research. Translation is investigated as a concept for future inquiry.

The book is expressive and formative of language-based research that is gaining momentum in business, management and organization research. It offers conceptual innovation through a thorough treatment of multilingualism and translation, having the potentiality to guide future empirical and theoretical research, and to dispel hidden hegemonic knowledge production practices. The readers will gain insights into the current status quo of language-based inquiry, discussions of multilingualism for research design and be informed about the philosophical underpinnings of language-based research. Specifically, the benefits include the review and summary of key publications in this field, discussion and analysis of hidden assumptions of knowledge production, a critical take on knowledge production, an outline and discussion of implications of multilingual research for research design and methods, discussion of philosophical underpinnings and a vision for future research.

The book is an invaluable source for all research students whose projects contain elements of multilingual research, whether empirical or theoretical. Likewise, the growing body of researchers who take a language-sensitive approach to their research may find it as a source that both 'pulls together' the current knowledge status quo while opening future trajectories for their projects. The book is extremely useful for the teaching of research methods in undergraduate, postgraduate and also master's or doctoral programmes as many students are not native English speakers and are directly confronted with the subject matter of the book.

Susanne Tietze, PhD, is Professor of Multilingual Management at Sheffield Business School, Sheffield Hallam University, UK. Her current research focuses on the constitution of multilingual organizations through language and translation.

State of the Art in Business Research
Series Editor: Geoffrey Wood

Recent advances in theory, methods and applied knowledge (alongside structural changes in the global economic ecosystem) have presented researchers with challenges in seeking to stay abreast of their fields and navigate new scholarly terrains.

State of the Art in Business Research presents shortform books which provide an expert map to guide readers through new and rapidly evolving areas of research. Each title will provide an overview of the area, a guide to the key literature and theories and time-saving summaries of how theory interacts with practice.

As a collection, these books provide a library of theoretical and conceptual insights, and exposure to novel research tools and applied knowledge, that aid and facilitate in defining the state of the art, as a foundation stone for a new generation of research.

Talent Management
A Research Overview
Anthony McDonnell and Sharna Wiblen

Language, Translation and Management Knowledge
A Research Overview
Susanne Tietze

Public Management
A Research Overview
Tom Entwistle

For more information about this series, please visit: www.routledge.com/State-of-the-Art-in-Business-Research/book-series/START

Language, Translation and Management Knowledge

A Research Overview

Susanne Tietze

LONDON AND NEW YORK

First published 2022
by Routledge
2 Park Square, Milton Park, Abingdon, Oxon OX14 4RN

and by Routledge
605 Third Avenue, New York, NY 10158

Routledge is an imprint of the Taylor & Francis Group, an informa business

British Library Cataloguing-in-Publication Data
A catalogue record for this book is available from the British Library

Library of Congress Cataloging-in-Publication Data
Names: Tietze, Susanne, author.
Title: Language, translation and management knowledge :
a research overview / Susanne Tietze.
Description: Abingdon, Oxon ; New York, NY : Routledge, 2022. |
Series: State of the art in business studies |
Includes bibliographical references and index.
Identifiers: LCCN 2021008552 (print) | LCCN 2021008553 (ebook)
Subjects: LCSH: Management–Research. | Management–Cross-cultural
studies–Research. | Multilingualism. | Translating and interpreting.
Classification: LCC HD30.4 .T497 2022 (print) |
LCC HD30.4 (ebook) | DDC 658/.049072–dc23
LC record available at https://lccn.loc.gov/2021008552
LC ebook record available at https://lccn.loc.gov/2021008553

ISBN: 978-0-367-35982-9 (hbk)
ISBN: 978-1-032-05844-3 (pbk)
ISBN: 978-0-429-34303-2 (ebk)

Typeset in Times New Roman
by Newgen Publishing UK

This book is dedicated to Dr David Campbell, bringer of merriment and mischief and inventor of words: *We ah snout!*

Contents

About the author

Susanne Tietze, PhD, MA, MBA, Teaching Dipl., is Professor of Multilingual Management at Sheffield Business School, Sheffield Hallam University, UK. Having studied in Germany, Switzerland and the UK, her contemporary research focuses on the exploration of the role of English, languages and translation in the production and exchange of management knowledge. She has recently concluded a research project funded by a UK Research Council, which investigated the agentic role of translators and interpreters as sense-makers and cultural facilitators in multilingual business communities.

Acknowledgements

I want to thank Tracey Coule, John McAuley and Vicky Welton for their help. I also want to acknowledge my long co-operation with Rebecca Piekkari: The dialogue and exchange with her has informed much of my thinking.

Abbreviations

BELF   Business English as a lingua franca
CCO   Communication as Constitutive of Organization
ELF   English as a lingua franca
MNC   Multinational corporations
PD   Prisoner's Dilemma [Game]
SI   Scandinavian Institutionalism

1   Introduction

Knowledge and understanding are intrinsically and inseparably linked to language. Global contexts are increasingly multilingual, and it thus becomes necessary to develop means and techniques to share knowledge across languages. Failing this, language use poses an immediate experience of a barrier to understanding: *Nessuna mia maestra a scuola, nessuna mia amica è stata mai incuriosita da fatto che io parlassi un'altra lingua* (Lahiri, 2016, p. 5). This quote translates as 'None of my teachers, none of my friends were ever curious about the fact that I spoke another language' (translated by Ann Goldstein). Without this translation readers of this sentence would not be able to make sense of it. Translation is thus a key language practice to understand how knowledge is shared across languages. Alternatively, a bridge language like English may well be used to establish a common ground. These practices are part and parcel of the themes and interests of this book as it asks the question: How knowledge is constructed and brought about in multilingual contexts?

In the opening pages of a book titled *Language, Translation and Management Knowledge. A Research Overview*, it makes sense to ponder what these terms mean and also to consider what it meant when such research is increasingly referred to as *international*. From thereon, further questions can be addressed: About how language and translation underpin international management research and whether to an extent language and translation are indeed central to it.

This book attempts to tackle issues pertaining to language(s) and translation in management research. In essence the view taken in this book is that languages and translation are indeed important points of departure for any research that crosses language boundaries, that is conducted by research teams of different cultural and language backgrounds and competencies or that relies on local mediating agents (e.g. to gain access) who operate in a local language, not spoken within the research team. This book may also be of interest to anyone who ever had to translate their empirical findings or their conceptual work into English – for purposes of publication or for gaining a degree. Academics who collect and analyse language data (in languages other than English in particular) will also find aspects of this book of interest. Finally, the book may also yield some insights for the guardians of knowledge and publications such as journal editors, critical readers or agents from publishing houses – as they, too, are part of the knowledge production process.

I am not a native English speaker, though my second professional socialization and education has been within UK universities and as such it was mediated through the English language to an extent that I can now 'perform' my academic trade in English. Overall, I found the ability or lack thereof to express my ideas and thoughts in English fascinating, disruptive and also incredibly helpful as working in this language continues to expose any false sense of the final 'say-so' in matters of research (as well as in teaching and the rest of life!). A feeling of strangeness remains whatever language I am operating in and, as a researcher with strong interpretative leanings, this decentredness is a helpful stance to question and query.

In this book, I will proceed to provide an overview of how research has developed responses and approaches to the language-based phenomena of international management from a language and translation perspective. In doing so, I will *zwei Fliegen mit einer Klappe schlagen* (as one would say in German) or 'kill two birds with one stone': I will problematize, briefly, how communities of management researchers have or have not responded to the phenomena of international management research and in doing so the themes of this book will emerge in such a way that they can be explored in subsequent chapters. That said, it is possible to read each chapter in its own right as central aspects, and arguments will be rehearsed in the context of each chapter. My sincere hope is that the readers of this book will become curious about language and translation.

The narrative tone used in this book is kept informal as far as this is possible in written academic accounts. This means I, as the author, am visible in these chapters and this is because working in and through the English language as a knowledge worker has been a challenge, a joy and a nuisance at times. In other words, the English language through which I conduct my research, and through which I order much of my personal and professional affairs, has been the shaping influence throughout my academic career, and consequently, articulating this influence as a legitimate and important research/knowledge issue has featured strongly in my academic Curriculum Vitae or my *Werdegang* (German), which loosely translates into the way one becomes something.

This informal tone will wax and wane throughout the book in line with the ideas that will be discussed; thus, the commentary of particular linguistic schools of thoughts or concomitant academic practices underpinned by philosophical assumptions will adhere to a more academic style of writing, with references to the extant literatures and examples taken from there.

The phenomena that are discussed in this book are how language and translation inform the knowledge production process and shape the available bodies of knowledge that are put in the world as reliable, valid or trustworthy and plausible accounts of the social world. The processes of knowledge production (research in academic contexts) and sharing (dissemination, mainly through written accounts) are carried in and through language. Therefore, it is important to understand how language is treated and used within the knowledge production process and beyond, i.e. the way how knowledge is presented to the world. In my view, both process and product are not neutral, value-free phenomena, but are inscribed with and grounded in assumptions about what makes for valid and useful knowledge and for whom and why. These meta-assumptions are rarely discussed within management research and in particular so, when it comes to research that is grounded in or involves languages other than English. In the words of Steyaert and Janssens (2013), I consider this to be a 'scandal', which needs addressing and is the main purpose of writing this book: I see the knowledge production process as a vested one, with deeply inscribed institutional and individual interests (Wilmot & Tietze, 2021, forthcoming). These can be rendered explicit through an investigation of the knowledge production process from a language and translation perspective.

Let's make a fuss: what is international management research?

I sometimes use the question 'What is international management research?' as an opening device for workshops, where I pose it to my students and the question sometimes results in a bit of bafflement as it is taken to be a 'given' that one knows of and engages in international management research without having to make much of a fuss about this. The answers that have been forthcoming in the past can be grouped as follows: International management research is characterized by (a) particular themes and topics such as, to name but a few, global supply chain management, dual career couples, international HRM or marketing or accounting, international alliances and joint ventures, knowledge transfer between MNC headquarters and subsidiaries, and global teams and how to manage them; (b) the comparative approach, i.e. any aspect, factor, variable or dimension that is different in different parts of the world and thus needs to be compared to each other; culture, in particular national cultural influences on business practices, is a favourite topic within this approach; (c) crossing borders and boundaries, i.e. any exchange of goods, services, people resources and other symbolic cultural resources that cross national borders or cultural boundaries; (d) being part of an international networks of academics and working in research teams; and (e) publishing in international journals.

In discussions with my students, we are able to establish that such crossing of boundaries, for example, brings people, ideas and practices together in such a way that results in an increase in diversity, dynamic movement and complexity as features that are shared throughout these different approaches, themes, comparisons and crossing of borders and boundaries. Frequently, students also point to the international focus (or global, as it is also referred to sometimes) as being the opposite of domestic (or local, as it is also referred to sometimes). Interestingly, students are very clear that it is somehow better to be international in focus and to become an international knowledge worker/academic as 'who wants to be only [sic] a domestic knowledge worker?' as one of my 'international' students once put it. Sometimes, students also express awareness that 'somehow' international and doing international business and management refer to practices from particular geopolitical parts of the world, viz. Anglo-American. This, interestingly, resonates with a perspective that has been expressed in particular in postcolonial, critical management studies, where being truly 'international' is often seen to be little more than referring to Anglo-American/Northern European business (Jack & Westwood, 2006).

The students provided good answers in my view – albeit sometimes slightly tautological, not just about the themes they identify as important and relevant but also about academic practices such as having international networks, being part of international research teams and publishing in international journals. These point to prevalent practices of being a management academic, and they are far from being neutral or objective practices, rather they are inscribed with values, preferences and notions of what constitutes valid knowledge (Lillis & Curry, 2014; Merliäinen, Tienari, Thomas & Davies, 2008). Of course, here the notion of using 'international' as a descriptor of what needs to be defined is somewhat tautological – but the repetitive and seemingly unavoidable, obvious and taken-for-granted use of the word 'international' points to the strong value that is attached to it and any practice that is associated with it. It is better to publish in an international journal (in particular US ones such as the selection of journals published by the Academy of Management) than in a domestic one. Right? And there are no choices for management academics to develop international themes, networks and approaches if they want an upwards trajectory in terms of their careers and professional standing – or are there?

Often, at this stage of the discussion, I ask students about the role of English in their research work and particularly international students [sic] comment strongly on its use as the language of writing, reading and where most of their concepts and frameworks come from. From these discussions with students, my own experience and research into these issues emerges the main gist of this book: The taken-for-granted assumptions about the use of the English language, the 'othering' of languages and the use of translation. Likewise, collective and institutional practices of using English as the sole acceptable language of management knowledge can and should be examined critically. The overall intent of this book is not to start a boycott of using English as a shared language, but to encourage the development of reflexive practices about how it is used in knowledge generation and dissemination.

Language and translation in international management research

The main focus in this book is on the role of languages, and in the first instance on the English language in the design, execution and writing of management research. The impact of English on the process and outcomes of research projects is an under acknowledged aspect of management research – under acknowledged, as it is taken for granted that research accounts are published in English – despite one feature of international management research being that it is located in different national, cultural contexts and that these include other language environments as well. This, in turn, necessitates translation *somewhere* within the overall research process. However, other than treating translation as a mechanistic problem to be resolved by back translation, there is little practice, let alone tradition, of providing explanatory commentary of how 'other' languages have been treated within research projects that include the generation of data in 'other' languages. Yet, even qualitative research fails to report on translation decisions taken (Chidlow, Plakoyiannaki & Welch, 2014, p. 571), and until very recently, there has been little interest in the role of (interlingual) translation in international management research (Piekkari, Tietze & Koskinen, 2020). In other words, the key argument in this book is that English, language

diversity and translation are *the* key hall mark of international management research as they are inevitable and practiced all the time; yet, all of
the language-based works remain in the 'black box' of the international
research process (Tietze, 2018).

That is not to say that roles of English, language diversity and translation have not been articulated at all within available literatures. Indeed,
in Chapters 3 and 4, in particular, these literatures will be summarized
and commented upon. Namely, language-sensitive international
business research (Piekkari & Tietze, 2011, p. 26) has been drawing
attention to the existence of language diversity and the dominant role
of English within multinational corporations (MNC) in particular for
several decades. Thus, there is an existing tradition of language-focused
research that explores international organizations (mainly, but not
exclusively, the MNC, Angouri & Piekkari, 2018) and examines how the
interplay of languages in use shapes organizational relationships, knowledge transfer and implementation of change. In this body of research,
which will be reviewed in Chapter 3, language diversity is central to
the thematic approaches developed in this field and conceptualizations
of using English and other languages have been developed (Steyaert,
Ostendorp & Gabrois, 2011).

Schools of thoughts, such as Scandinavian Institutionalism (SI),
have engaged with the travel of ideas and practices around the globe,
and why and how they change when they arrive in specific locations.
These scholars have used the notion of metaphorical translation and
define it as the 'modification that a practice or an idea undergoes
when it is implemented in a new organizational context' (Boxenbaum
& Strandgaard Pedersen, 2009, pp. 190–191). From thereon they have
contributed to articulating the role and influence of local agents who
shape incoming ideas and practices (Czarniawska & Sevón, 1996, 2005).
Scholars within the school of thought, called glocalization, see the local
and the global in a mutually constitutive relationship with glocalizing
agents being positioned at the interstices of translation between the
global and the local. They draw on their discursive resources to influence
the reception of fusion process of practice across time, space, border
and boundaries (Drori, Höllerer & Walgenbach, 2014, p. 92). Thus,
local recontextualization of incoming practices is achieved, amongst
others, also through translation. Likewise, Organization Studies have
developed approaches to understanding processes of organization
that draw heavily on an understanding of language as discourse in
use: Communication as Constitutive of Organization (CCO) is perhaps the most prominent of language-sensitive approaches as it views
organizations as communicated into being through ongoing, interacting

and fluid acts of communication, i.e. as discursive action, which sees 'communication as constitutive of meaning (and thus of organizational reality) [and] positions communication as a vital *explanation for* organizational phenomena' (Cooren, Taylor & van Every, 2006; Schoeneborn, Kuhn & Kärreman, 2019, p. 476, *italics* in the original) and for discursively understood institutional phenomena (Schmidt, 2008).

There are therefore traditions and approaches within management studies that provide rich knowledge about the importance of how language is used, by whom, in which contexts and to what consequences. These include also international contexts where language diversity is contributing to the complexities of communicating, meaning making and sense giving. Yet, mainly, organization and management studies, CCO, SI and glocalization literatures are monolingual in that English remains their only language of publication and language data other than that which gets translated into English remains invisible in most of their respective research accounts. The literature deriving from international business studies and focused on language issues in contrast has a stronger multilingual orientation but continues to exist in relative isolation from the other fields of inquiry (see Karhunen, Louhiala-Salminen, Kankaanranta & Piekkari, 2018; Tenzer, Terjesen & Harzing, 2017; Tietze & Piekkari, 2020).

A second aim of this book is therefore to advocate a stronger alignment between management literatures that have all embraced language and communication as central to processes of organizing. They also share an underpinning philosophy in which language is seen as performative of social actions and an important discursive resource available to different individual and collective actors. It is the argument of this book that in international contexts, such communicative organizing inevitably involves English as well as other languages and translation, and it is therefore important to include them more deliberately into international management research itself and in the wider process of knowledge production.

And finally, an answer

So, what is international management research? In summarizing the thoughts developed by my students, fellow researchers and myself, it is research that takes a non-domestic point of view about its topics and themes and acknowledges the nexus of ties between language and knowledge. It is disseminated (published) in the English language but includes reflection about empirical data or conceptual frameworks taken from languages other than English. It acknowledges and articulates therefore the existence and role of translation in the research process.

How will the chapters unfold?

The overall purpose of the book is to investigate knowledge production processes from a language and translation perspective and pay heed to hidden phenomena such as vested interests and power relations inscribed in the scholarly (institutional) production process. In Chapter 2, the contemporary global language of knowledge, English, is investigated from this perspective. Chapter 3 contains a consideration of language diversity and translation as part of the knowledge production process. Chapter 4 discusses the nexus of ties between English, language diversity and translation. Chapter 5 discusses how the development of global literacies require sensitivity and knowledge about the writing process. Chapter 6 advocates the integration of language and translation into the written text production within management studies.

In detail, the chapters' content is outlined below:

In Chapter 2, *English and Management Research,* the focus of attention is on the English language. It is investigated as a particular *code* that orders knowledge in a particular way. At the same time, it is pointed out that each language codes knowledge in its own unique way – this is called linguistic relativity, and it explains why writing in English also provides a particular *perspective* onto the world and its affairs. Therefore, mistaking English for a universal language that can code all possible knowledge is problematic as inscribed in such an understanding is an essentialist perspective on language. Finally, the use of English is a dominant, taken-for-granted *practice* in the management academy, and it can result in the enactment of hegemonic relationships and knowledge: The worldviews that privileges English data over that of other language data and thereby also orders the relationship between researchers and their different cultural and language traditions accordingly (Meriläinen *et al.*, 2008; Tietze & Dick, 2013).

Chapter 3, *English, Language Diversity and Translation in Management Research*, introduces several bodies of literature, albeit briefly, that have engaged with language either as discourse or as language-in-use or indeed with translation. Translation understood as part of sense-making within the same language is called *intralingual translation* and this approach has been espoused by some schools of thoughts within management and organization research, for example, the organizational change literature draws on this notion of translation. This approach is contrasted with *interlingual translation*, where translation is seen as the process of meaning change from one language to another. This approach has been espoused in particular by language-sensitive international business and management literature. It is, in concluding, advocated that both notions of translation need to be drawn together in order to reap its full analytic potential.

Chapter 4, *Towards a Reconfiguration of Language Diversity and Translation in Management Research*, focuses on some critical management literature and discusses the consequences of using English as the dominant language of management knowledge in an unreflexive way for knowledge thus created. Examples are provided of how the use of English impacts on the important aspects of the research process, from generating initial ideas, to data analysis and so forth. Examples of practices and research that contribute to a more comprehensive use of language diversity and translation are provided throughout the chapter.

Chapter 5, *Developing Global Literacy for Management Research*, brings together some of the questions that have been raised in previous chapters. Some examples of what it means to write from a position of global literacy are introduced and these provide a blueprint to develop writing strategies that are aimed at including, theorizing and embracing the 'other', whether understood as a language, cultural or political other. Translation is regarded as a means to exercise hospitality within encounters of 'self' and 'other'.

Chapter 6, *Conclusion: On Being Spoken and Being Written*, returns to a consideration, play and reversal on grammatical structure and normative order that was introduced in Chapter 2, viz. that language 'speaks us', rather than that we speak language. Likewise, it is proposed that texts write us, rather than that we write texts. This concetto enables a final reflection about the (assumed) role of agency and authorship in the production of academic (English language) texts, whereas the reversal of the grammatical order acts as an invitation to engage in a reflexive achievement of agency through writing, rather than a presupposed and exaggerated notion of the author as a free-wielding agent.

References

Angouri, J. and Piekkari, R. (2018). Organising multilingually: Setting an agenda for studying language at work. *European Journal of International Management*, *12*, 1–2, 8–27.

Boxenbaum, E. and Strandgaard Pedersen, J. (2009). Scandinavian institutionalism: A case of institutional work. In T. B. Lawrence, R. Suddaby, and B. Leca (Eds.). *Institutional work: Actors and agency in institutional studies of organization*, (pp. 178–204). Cambridge, UK: Cambridge University Press.

Chidlow, A., Plakoyiannaki, E. and Welch, C. (2014). Translation in cross-language international business research: Beyond equivalence. *Journal of International Business Studies, 45*, 562–582.

Cooren, F., Taylor, J. R. and van Every, E. J. (2006). *Communication as organizing. Empirical and theoretical explorations in the dynamic of text and conversation.* Mahwah, NJ: Lawrence Erlbaum Associates.

Czarniawska, B. and Sevón, G. (1996). *Translating organizational change.* Berlin, Germany: de Gruyter.

Czarniawska, B. and Sevón, G. (2005). *Global ideas: How ideas, objects and practices travel in the global economy.* Copenhagen, Denmark: Liber & Copenhagen Business School Press.

Drori, G. S., Höllerer, M. A. and Walgenbach, P. (2014). *Global themes and local variations in organization and management: Perspectives on glocalization.* New York, NY: Routledge.

Jack, G. and Westwood, R. (2006). Postcolonialism and the politics of qualitative research in international business, *Management International Review, 46*, 4, 481–501.

Karhunen, P., Louhiala-Salminen, L., Kankaanranta, A. and Piekkari, R. (2018). Let's talk about language: A review of language-sensitive research in international management, *Journal of Management Studies, 55*, 6, 980–1013.

Lahiri, J. (2016). *In other words.* London, UK: Bloomsbury Publishing.

Lillis, T. and Curry, J. (2014). *Academic writing in a global context. The politics and practices of publishing in English.* London, UK: Taylor and Francis.

Meriläinen, S., Tienari, J., Thomas, R. and Davies, A. (2008). Hegemonic academic practices: Experiences from publishing from the periphery, *Organization, 15*, 4, 584–597.

Piekkari, R. and Tietze, S. (2011). A world of languages: Implications for international management research and practice, *Journal of World Business, 46*, 3, 267–269.

Piekkari, R., Tietze, S. and Koskinen, K. (2020). Metaphorical and interlingual translation in moving organizational practices across languages, *Organization Studies, 9*, 1311–1332.

Schmidt, V. (2008). Discursive institutionalism. The explanatory power of ideas and discourse. *Annual Review of Political Sciences, 11*, 303–326.

Schoeneborn, D., Kuhn, T. and Kärreman, D. (2019). The communicative constitution of organization, organizing, and organizationality. *Organization Studies, 40*, 475–496.

Steyaert, C. and Janssens, M. (2013). Multilingual scholarship and the paradox of translation and language in management and organization studies. *Organization, 20*, 131–142.

Steyaert, C., Ostendorp, A. and Gabrois, C. (2011). Multilingual organizations as 'linguascapes': Negotiating the position of English through discursive practices, *Journal of World Business, 46*, 270–278.

Tenzer, H., Terjesen, S. and Harzing, A. W. (2017). Language in international business research: A review and agenda for future research. *Management International Review, 57*, 6, 815–854.

Tietze, S. (2018). Multilingual research, monolingual publications: Management scholarship in English only? *European Journal of International Management*, *12*, 28–45.

Tietze, S. and Dick, P. (2013). The victorious English language: Hegemonic practices in the management academy. *Journal of Management Inquiry*, *22*, 122–134.

Tietze, S. and Piekkari, P. (2020). Languages and cross-cultural management. In B. Szkudlarek, L. Roman, D. V. Caprar and J. S. Osland (Eds.). *The Sage handbook of contemporary cross-cultural management*, (pp. 424–438). London and Thousand Oaks: Sage.

Wilmot, N. and Tietze, S. (2021, forthcoming). Englishization and the politics of translation. *Critical Perspectives on International Business*. https://doi.org/10.1108/cpoib-03-2020-0019

2 English and management research

Barbara Ehrenreich, a social activist, undercover journalist, describes the link between reality and words in her biography: '... another language is therefore losing your grip on reality. That is why it is so hard, so soul-destroying if not resolved, so liberating, if understood' (Ehrenreich, 2014, p. 137).

In this chapter the English language will be discussed in terms of its status as the global language of management knowledge, how this status also provides perspectives on knowledge and how this leads to particular practices – institutional, organizational and individual – that promulgate particular intellectual dispositions about the usefulness and validity of knowledge thus created. However, the unquestioned use of English may also cause non-native speakers a sense of profound lack of expression of their research and their findings, thus losing the grip on reality that is expected of academic knowledge workers.

The rise and rise of English?

The English language has become the global *lingua franca* of science and knowledge (Lillis & Curry, 2014; Montgomery, 2013; Wierzbicka, 2014). A *lingua franca* is a free language at the disposal of everyone who wants to use it, and it enables communication between speakers of different languages. It is a foreign language to both speakers (see Vandermeeren, 1999), and it makes possible the sharing of ideas, stories, thoughts and experiences. It has also been described as a bridging language that enables communications between speakers of different languages. There have been many different *lingua francas* throughout history (see Ostler, 2005), and it is unlikely that English will keep this status for ever (Janssens & Steyaert, 2014; Ostler, 2010).

Indeed, the contemporary dominance of English is historically an important point of departure that occurred at the time when 'English speakers begin to travel and settle abroad [...] the world is opened up to the English but above all to their business and trading enterprise' (Ostler, 2005, pp. 114–115). Thus, English was from early on the language used to coin terms for trade and commerce and establish relationships amongst trading parties. Ostler tracks the current status of English as a global language originating from the first voyages of the East Indian Company in 1591 with long-term results including that it was established as a language of business and education through colonialism to its roll out across the world after the Second World War as the language of global institutions and the commercial as well as cultural strength of the US in the twentieth century (Crystal, 2003). Thus, the use of language and decisions about which language to use for global communications is reflective of the wider political-historical developments and influences (Phillipson, 2009).

Philippson (1992, p. 72) has articulated the power dimensions of language choice by coining the term (English language) *linguistic imperialism*, which he defines as:

> [t]he dominance of English [is] asserted and maintained by the establishment and continuous reconstitution of structural and cultural inequalities between English and other languages. Here structure refers broadly to material properties (for example, institutions, financial allocations) and cultural to immaterial or ideological properties (for example, attitudes, pedagogic principles).

Thus, the use of English is constitutive of particular historic-political constellations of power, which continue to shape institutional process and the location of individuals in it, i.e. to which extent, for example, they are able to marshal English to access funds or to teach in English as the preferred language – the ideological logics that underpin the structures of systems are also manifest in the use of language. The spread of global English serves the vested interest of trade, commerce and capitalist structures – a case in point made by Halliday (2003, p. 408) who sees global English as expressive of taxonomic orders of meanings, new forms of knowledge, with 'their own ways of reasoning and arguing, of presenting and marshalling lines of information and control'. However, scholars like Crystal (2003) point to the beneficial aspects of having a shared code (a *lingua franca*) as an effective means to create cultures of mutual intelligibility, where sometimes individuals and collectives may struggle to gain access to it or gain proficiency, but which overall serves as a beneficial means of achieving commercial, political and cultural ends.

Notwithstanding these different positions' vis-à-vis the use and status of English as a global *lingua franca*, it is the language of knowledge and science (Montgomery, 2013) as any aspiration by knowledge workers to partake in global knowledge networks is dependent on having recourse to using English. Questions of whether this is the continuation and perpetual reconstitutions of (neo)colonial relationships and vested interests, whether its use shapes the perspectives on knowledge that are created, and whether it is a fair and equitable to impose English, even if indirectly, will be addressed in the remainder of this chapter. First, however, one main interest of this book will be discussed: The nexus of ties between knowledge and language, perspectives on knowledge and language and what this means for collective and individual practice in the management academy.

Language and knowledge

Language can be seen as a system in which knowledge is coded: Signs (words, concepts) are ordered in a particular way (grammar) so that through their relationship it is possible to describe and explain the material and social world. Words and concepts (and whole texts) make up our vocabularies and they are carriers of meanings. Such meanings and how they are tied to their conceptual expressions are based on human agreement, which is collectively passed on through socialization processes. For example, the meaning of the word 'tree' *refers* to an object that grows from the earth, has leaves, provides shade, etc. There is nothing 'tree-like' as such in the object one refers to when using the word tree. Indeed, when using the word tree, one uses culturally agreed sequences of sounds and letters, in a culturally agreed order: The tree provides shade; but not: Shade provides the tree. These functions of language are called the referential function of language – in contrast to the essentialist thinking which assume that language expresses a tree-like reality.

Language is a cultural ordering code and is based on human agreement. Therefore, it entails the possibility to disagree, to challenge and to create new meanings. This is perhaps more obvious with more abstract concepts such as leadership or strategy and the questions of what they refer to and what they stand for. The second function of language is, therefore, that it enables human beings to *abstract* themselves from concrete immediacies and locate themselves in a more flexible, transportable and more symbolic manner.

These referential, symbolic and abstracting features of language have made it possible for information to be communicated across time and space. However, each language codes knowledge and thereby the understanding and construction of (social) world in different ways. If languages are related, the differences are sometimes not very dramatic, but if languages are historically and geographically apart, the coding of the world through words can differ immensely.

Linguistic relativity

According to anthropological linguist Alessandro Duranti (2000, p. 220) languages 'provide different ways of describing the world', because each language establishes a meaning system that is not totally commensurable with that of another language. Native speakers of one language therefore may see the word differently from speakers of another language and respond and make sense of it in different ways. This difference between languages has been theorized as *linguistic relativity*, an expression also known as the Sapir–Whorf hypothesis (despite these two scholars never making a shared statement about it). The linguist and anthropologist Sapir (1949, p. 161) defined it as follows:

> The real world is to a large extent unconsciously built up on the language habits of the group. No two languages are ever sufficiently similar to be considered as representing the same social reality. The worlds in which different societies live are distinct worlds, not merely the same world with different labels attached.

Sapir stresses here the difference between languages and how, therefore, social realities are constructed differently in each language – he does not talk about total incommensurability between languages, nor does he propose that language determines the respective perspectives of different native speaker groups. Such a stance would be associated with what is called *linguistic determinism* – in which language would be like a prison cell from which there is no escape (Agar, 1994).

Linguistic relativity proposes that the native language of a speaker shapes, provides colour and nuance to how reality is seen and described; language also informs what is being paid attention to (this may influence decisions about the selection of research topics and research questions), how it is understood (this may influence the conceptual framing of data or the whole research project) and what is seen as relevant and important (this may influence data analysis and selection of which data is selected to feature in written research accounts). Language is then very much part of our bounded rationality, which shapes our ability to cognitively understand the social world from an inclusive, all comprehensive perspective. However, within the traditions of management and business research, this language-boundedness is neither acknowledged nor does it get addressed. This is not to say that it cannot be addressed at all – indeed as it will be argued later, it can, creatively, be integrated into the research process – as it is possible to translate between languages. If this were not possible at all, total incommensurability between meaning systems would prevail and communication across languages would be impossible (see Agar, 1994).

The consequences of linguistic relativity for business and management studies that are dominated by English (Steyaert & Janssens, 2013) have rarely been articulated or scrutinized within respective scholarly communities. In the following, three rare examples from business and management studies are presented, which demonstrate how and why language is so important to set the parameters for practice, behaviour and conceptualizations.

Manzella (2019) investigates the particular aspects of employee relations from a language and translation perspective, viz. the Italian notion of *caporalato* (or *caporale*) and how it is translated into English in official documents. These terms define individuals who organize casual labour, often seasonal, and come from a historical personage from feudal southern Italy connoted with brutality and exploitation. Nowadays it denotes the archetypal labour trafficker (Manzella, 2019, p. 110) and within Italian law it is an illegal form of intermediation. In English these translate into *gangmaster systems* and *gangmasters*.

Within the English legislative system, the activities of gangmasters now refer to legal, licence-depending intermediate activities. The incident that prompted a change in legislation was a tragedy of 23 seasonal Chinese illegal migrant workers drowning or dying of hyperthermia when collecting cockles at Morecambe Bay in 2004. These labourers were hired and organized through a gangmaster system, which had remained mainly unregulated till then and exploited in particular the vulnerabilities of illegal migrant work forces. Following a gangmaster licencing act, gangmasters' roles have become legalized in the provision of casual labour, conditioned on the receipt of a licence. This change in legal practice does not convey the source meaning anymore and is problematic in that in Italy, *caporali* still operate outside the law. "Gangmaster" then can become a misnomer, as it expresses 'the opposite meaning to *caporali*' (Manzella, 2019, p. 113). Thus, from an Italian perspective the immediate meaning of *caporali* remains unchanged and refers to criminal activity, whereas in the UK employment relations system, the meaning has been changed.

Translators would have to explain such changes of meanings as the literally translated word (*caporali* – *Gangmaster*) now entails different perspectives on the law – or lawlessness.

An experimental study by Akkerman, Harzing and van Witteloostuijn (2010) used a famous experiment called the 'Prisoner's Dilemma Game'. It is taken from game theory, and it is based on the notion that two rational individuals may not cooperate even if it appears to be in their best interest to do so. The study is based on an experimental set-up in which Dutch students, who had previously lived within an Anglophone culture and thus had a strong exposure to the English language, played the Prisoner's Dilemma (PD) game. Results showed that 'playing the PD game in English has a significantly negative impact on the number of cooperative choices' (p. 574), and that students responded more competitively when enacting this experiment in English (as compared to Dutch).

As the English language is seen to enable speakers to express more strongly assertiveness, achievement and individualistic orientation, it also primes behaviour in line with these values. The authors state that

> our results reveal that playing a PD game in English has a significantly negative impact on the number of cooperative choices. This result shows that the weak version of the Sapir-Whorf hypothesis (Crystal, 2002), which argues that language influences the way we think, might possibly be expanded to including behaviour as well as thought.
>
> (p. 574)

Gaggiotti and Marre's (2017) organizational ethnography (located within a Italo-Latin-American multinational corporation) demonstrates how leadership vocabulary is highly resonant with historical meanings and that words like leader (e.g. *duce* and *caudillo*) are avoided by organizational members; this is partly so as they are associated with violent, authoritative and antidemocratic leadership, but also because a lexical loan word from English (here the vocabulary of leader and leadership) fails to express the complexities of leadership within multilingual organizations. Instead, loan words were used depending on the context speakers were in and their assessment whether these words were useful in what they meant to achieve. Their use could assist in avoiding any association with domineering practices and were action-oriented and not based on abstract notions of leading.

The studies briefly reviewed here are quite different in terms of their methodology (general investigation of legal terminology and translation, a quasi-experimental study and an organizational ethnography). The approaches range from discussing language-related aspects of (translation) practices and meaning, to the link between language use and behavioural choices and the responses and sense-making of the vocabulary and meaning of leadership when used as a polyphonically loan word. Thus, notwithstanding the differences between the three studies, they are underpinned by a common perspective on language which is alignable with the principles of linguistic relativity as words/concepts are shown as malleable, polyphonic, used in context and informing dispositions to act or otherwise in particular ways. Some management literatures have begun to engage with these subject matters. A summary of these developments will be presented in Chapter 3.

English: a powerful code and practice

Language is a culturally grounded meaning and ordering system – operationalized through words and grammar – that can stabilize meanings only to an extent and which therefore is also characterized by flexibility, fluidity and opens up the possibility of resisting, challenging and rejecting any given system of meaning and order. As was shown in the discussion of three recent studies, language uses 'primes' behaviour and actions in the world as it comes with perspective, worldviews and dispositions that become enacted in contexts-of-use.

In terms of international management and business research, English is the dominant code that reflects the briefly outlined historical developments propelling English into the status quo of a global (knowledge) *lingua franca*. Cultural-institutional practices have been developed that are rooted in English-only language use. In other words, the (tacit) expectation is that knowledge is to be disseminated and communicated only through the English language. However, from the point of view of linguistic relativity, this is problematic, as the English language carries with it particular perspectives on and dispositions towards the world that are different from other languages. These 'other' languages and perspectives tend to get treated as a problem to be translated away through quite a mechanistic use of back translation (Chidlow, Plakiannayi & Welch, 2014) or they get not acknowledged at all and disappear in a black box of management research (Tietze, 2018).

The use of English is not in itself problematic. Indeed, it has enabled the sharing of knowledge across languages, cultures, nation states, and it forms the basis of knowledge networks and research collaborations that otherwise could not take place or would have to rely on translation, which can take spontaneity out of the process. An orientation towards using

English is therefore plausible and useful. The use of English as such is not the object of debate here; rather it is its use as the taken-for-granted, tacit and exclusive means of creating and disseminating management.

Using English in such a way is based on an assumption that it is *universal* in character and as such has inherent qualities that enable it to express all possible knowledge within all possible (business/management) situations and contexts. Concomitantly attributing universal descriptive and expressive powers to English are assumptions of it being able to express essential meanings. English is treated as *xenoglossia* (perfect understanding regardless of a multitude of languages) insofar as ambiguities or loss of meaning through translation are seen as solvable (Czarniawska, 1999). For example, the terms leader and leadership from a xenoglossic perspective express stable meanings that remain the same even if used in different contexts as they express something essential about leaders and leadership. While literatures have made progress in terms of taking a more sophisticated view on leadership (e.g. Schedliztki, Ahonen, Edwards & Gaggiotti, 2016) through investigating the contingencies of leadership or through framing it as situated, malleable enactment within leader–follower relationships, it is yet to engage more fully with language perspectives on leadership and how this very bendable concept plays into different enactments.

English as practice

There are consequences for the unacknowledged and unexamined use of English as if it were the only, the best and the most obvious language of all (management/business) knowledge. As the world of words and the world of actions are interlinked, it is appropriate to consider some consequences of using English in this way as it is the dominant knowledge practice in the management academy.

English and knowledge workers

Management academics are knowledge workers who are engaged in the creation and dissemination of knowledge through their symbolic-analytic work (Reich, 2001). In this regard they are agents who shape the currents of knowledge that flow through global networks and that form the conduit and shape the contours of the global knowledge economy. They deal in symbols such as words and figures and they analyse them – i.e. they manipulate information in such a way to create and contribute to (mobile) bodies of knowledge. Their success or failure to do this is therefore directly related to their ability to use language as the knowledge they absorb, create and release back into the world is packed into language.

In a time of mobile knowledge networks, it is packed in the English language. Therefore, the ability to partake and find standing and success in a global academic market place is directly contingent on the knowledge worker's ability to not only speak or communicate in English but also exercise a degree of mastery and control over it (Tietze, 2009). Inscribed into global academic knowledge systems is a reliance on the English language as the appropriate 'transport mechanism' so to speak. This is presupposed on quite problematic assumptions of equal and consistent access to English (see Canagarajah, 1996; Flowerdew, 2000), all of which are themes in literatures on the sociopolitics of languages and in particular English as the global language of choice.

Within the management and business fields of inquiry, there exist by now a handful of studies that document how the use of English, if remaining unexamined, can be a hegemonic practice (Meriläinen, Tienari, Thomas & Davies, 2008) that perpetuates centre-peripheral relationships within research collaborations and that shapes career trajectories of management academics.

Meriläinen *et al.* (2008) report from the experience of a Finnish-British research team consisting of four respected senior academics – two from Finland and two from Great Britain – who joined forces to examine the phenomenon of consultancy understood as particular societal discourses. Through a self-examination of their cross-cultural research engagement, these academics show how hegemonic practices as prevalent in the institutional academic structures (e.g. through journal ranking lists, performance measurement) are reconstituted through their enactment in micro, everyday exchanges and communications. This is shown to reinforce and constitutive core-peripheral relationships between different centres of management knowledge, with the US – and thus being able to express one's ideas in English – being the most dominant one (Macdonald & Kam, 2007). Hegemony comes into play as it relates to power issues and the domination of one class or group over another through the exercise of normative control. It is less obvious and blatant than the physical-coercive exercise of power, as it works through the control of values and beliefs that are transferred mainly through social-political and occupational socialization.

Through narrating the story of how a written research account was developed, the authors describe the crux of the argument as related to language and translation issues that coloured the knowledge production within this research team:

the problem of having texts translated into English on the assumption that it represents a global lingua franca. However, the translation (and thus decontextualization) of language-in-use is problematic. Translation is often achieved at the expense of a loss of meaning for those aspects of 'untranslatability' of localized voices. The tendency of users of the English language to assume that its structure and rules reflect some natural and objective reality results in a lack of recognition of playing down of the different realities afforded by different languages.

(Meriläinen *et al.*, 2008, p. 592)

The account provided theorizes a variety of seemingly mundane and trivial practices (e.g. which data to present at conferences) amongst four research collaborators as recurring actions through which core-peripheral relationships are reconstituted and cemented as normal and preferable – with representatives of the periphery (here Finnish) actively participating in their own 'othering' through offering their data as interesting examples if compared to the central and therefore normalized ideas and positions of the core of management knowledge production (here British).

In a follow-on piece (Thomas, Tienari, Davies & Meriläinen, 2009), the authors deepen the reflexive gaze on their research collaboration and review their practices through 'radical reflexivity' (p. 316), an inter-rogation of how and why truth claims are made not only in terms of questions of research design but also includes questions of how and why research accounts are written and by whom. Differences between the British and Finnish participants are again played out in mundane decisions about the interviewing schedules, meanings and interpretation of data references to gender/sex, and how they are made sense of as this distinction highlights the linguistically contingent and situated char-acter of concepts.

The paper shows how the historical-geographical location of the four researchers shaped their interpretations of the research interviews and made them predisposed towards conducting the data collection process in different ways. English was the language used for their exchanges and for the writing of research accounts, and therefore, it is indeed an enabler of this particular research collaboration. At the same time, it also caused conflict of an epistemological and political nature. It brought to the fore struggles: Struggles about which readings or which data were considered to be important and relevant as it became mani-fest in the selection of data at presentations for conferences.

While the centre-periphery relations in the project and experiences of the Finnish-British collaboration were addressed and resolved through self-reflexive practice, other accounts of Englishization of the production of management knowledge point to the continuation and acceleration of English-language dominance and its consequences. Boussebaa and Brown (2017) argue that the Englishization in management knowledge production 'is ultimately "remaking" locals as Anglophones through a quasi-voluntary process of imperialism in the context of US-dominated era of "globalization" and "global English"' (p. 7). They see the adoption of English as a disciplinary process, whereby management academics exercise self-discipline in the adoption of English as their main knowledge language.

Progressively, this exercise of self-discipline begins to shape their identities as well. Their empirical study is located within French universities/business schools, which provides an interesting case setting in the light of the strong identification of French people with their language and its protection by law. French business schools are seen to be situated within a context of globalization and international competition between providers of higher education services. However, Englishization is not just externally imposed; 'it is also the product of conformist (self-disciplining) identities at the individual level' (p. 24) with individual academics making decisions about where to locate themselves on a spectrum of possibilities of complying with, adjusting to, or rejecting Anglophone identities and its hallmark of writing, publishing (and thinking) in English.

Boussebaa and Brown (2017) also point to some mediating factors in this language-identity work: The age of management academics being significant (with younger academics being more open to using English) and the disciplinary sub-field, where some fields such as economics have embraced the use of English for many decades, whereas other fields such as industrial sociology have not.

Tietze and Dick (2013) provide an account of how non-native English-speaking management academics located in European business schools cope with the expected use of English as the language of management knowledge. Decisions to embrace or avoid the use of English are closely tied to academics' self-perceptions about their ability to generate and express knowledge in English and the concomitant pressure that without this ability access to and success within institutional and community structures cannot be achieved. Depending on the relative position of academics with regard to requiring entry, being positioned in mid-career or later career roles, the study differentiates between willing players (either post-doctoral students or early career academics), reluctant and compliant players (mid-career academics) and liberated players located in the last third of their employment at university. The willing players were under the strongest pressure to develop competence in working at near-native speaker level with the English language.

They also amended or changed their research topics to make it more palatable to journal editors in particular. For example, one interviewee stated that publications needed to be in certain journals in order for him to be successful in gaining a permanent position. He described his own research focus as too local and commented further that he would have to be better at English and in finding a more interesting perspective on his work. Willing players also offered themselves as labourers for more experienced colleagues in return for help with publications, or for being integrated into (English language) networks. Reluctant or compliant players are securely settled in their organizational positions, but often are disconcerted by the newly introduced performance management practices (e.g. a point system that differentiated between different kinds of publications with those in English language journals overall attracting higher scores). They also want to attain career progression and in order to attain it, they had to display dispositions and practices in line with what Boussebaa and Brown (2017) call a quasi-voluntary subjection to the (hegemonic) demands to think and work in English, to align topics of research accordingly, matching the expectations of centres of knowledge production. There was awareness of being thus subjected and some academics resisted the performance management systems that encouraged a particular behaviour, e.g. by ensuring that they continued to publish in their native language to reach local audiences.

Yet, all academics complied to an extent as it is important for them to have the respect of and good standing within their institution, to be successful in gaining promotion or other rewards, as they had also accepted that English is the language of knowledge in their own university and far beyond. Thus, participation in English language knowledge production was also seen as inevitable and useful to an extent. Senior academics, having less to lose, were the most liberated players and sometimes dared to challenge the system – e.g. by not adhering completely to the parameters of performance management systems and refusing to discriminate against colleagues who do not publish in English.

English and the production of knowledge

Consequences of using a language in a hegemonic manner have been shown to affect the (re)constitutions of identities of knowledge workers; whether they are in favourable positions to do so makes a difference in their professional success and standing as well as their personal well-being and material security (Boussebaa & Brown, 2017; Tietze & Dick, 2013). In addition to the effects on knowledge workers' identities, there are also effects on the kind of knowledge that is produced and found to be relevant and valid – which of course raises the question, relevant for whom and considered valid by whom?

Postcolonial studies provide an answer in terms of which geographical centres are powerful in setting agendas and providing perspectives on what counts as rigorous research and valid knowledge. Grey (2010) points to North American influence, in particular in practices pertaining to journal publications and journal ranking lists. Üsdiken (2010) demonstrates that the core of management knowledge production is located in the US and why it has become the main source of influence over knowledge production since the Second World War; a secondary centre is the UK and there are semi-peripheral Western and Northern European countries and a periphery of Southern and Eastern Europe.

It could be argued that such an order of knowledge centres overlaps strongly with the model of concentric circles offered more than 30 years ago by Kachru (1986) who explored the power of English language and its colonizing effects on countries. The inner circle countries comprise nations such as the UK and the US, whereas the outer circle countries are former colonial sites such as India, Singapore and Nigeria where English is a second or official language. Expanding circles of English language users are increasingly using English as a foreign language, in particular in education, commerce as well as science and scholarship.

The English language, so the argument goes, continues to be used by educated elite groups in societies who have access to it, and also by increasing mobile knowledge workers who can take their knowledge coded in English with them and make it available elsewhere. Fears of English dominating the whole fields of knowledge and pushing out other languages have been expressed as *diglossia*. For example, Ljosland (2007) describes how English is increasingly being used in the training of young researchers across many academic disciplines to an extent that whole knowledge domains are mentally occupied by English where Norwegian could equally be used. Thus the use of English becomes normalized, indeed preferred, as the language of progress and prestige.

In business and management there is almost no choice available if a knowledge worker wants to be successful in their field of specialism. Indeed, English has shaped the vocabularies and meanings of business and management discourses in a deep and lasting way – to an extent that management scholarship needs to focus on which domains of management and business studies are mainly researchable and comprehensible through the English language, and which are not.

The study by a and x about loan words for leadership is an example for the foreign (i.e. non-English) word left visible, which in turn enables the authors to point to the non-totalizing aspects of the leadership discourse as leadership is shown to be situated and historically located rather than a universal-total concept.

Choices made by individual scholars occur within particular organizational and institutional environments. Boussebaa and Brown (2017) and Tietze and Dick (2013) point to the role of organizational performance management systems, such as rewarding publications in English language journals, in particular those associated with prestige outlets such as journals ranked in specific journal ranking lists or in the *Financial Times*. In particular, getting tenure and achieving stable and continued employment (tenure systems in some universities) are of crucial importance for young academics, the willing players, whose very existence may be dependent on gaining entry into the academy.

Individuals are responding to such pressure on a continuum between total compliance and some resistance. Organizational practices channel such choices and reward particular behaviours that are all linked to English-language practices. Boussebaa and Tienari (2019) discuss Englishization in terms of the politics of knowledge production in management studies. Their main argument is that US-dominated journal ranking lists are used in business schools to assess individuals' merit as knowledge workers and that this creates a 'monoculture and reconstituting other forms of scholarship as marginal and inferior' (p. 5). Consequently, knowledge itself becomes homogenized and produces significant 'language-based inequalities and [inducing] demanding quasi-colonial forms of identity work for this being Englishized' (p. 5).

Organizational practices include the entry (and later promotion) of applicants based on their track record or potential in publishing in journals listed in the *Financial Times* 50 or journals rated four stars in the academic journal guides, e.g. Chartered Association of Business Schools in the UK. Invariably, the journals are English-language journals. Reward systems such as payment of bonuses are based on successful publication in these 'top journals' and good representation of staff's publications in them will impress accreditation bodies and their representatives.

Furthermore, there are many other practices which shape the production of knowledge. For example, developmental workshops about learning how to write for the right journals are offered as a matter of routine at doctoral colloquia, conference workshops cater to similar needs, meet-the-editor meetings and mentoring initiatives are offered to enable access to people and skills and further the development of internal dispositions (with networking skills and resilience being currently fashionable). These are organizational-institutional practices that not only channel knowledge production, but also shape the kind of knowledge that is being generated in terms of authors working hard to create a perspective that is not only interesting to journal editors in the first instance but also impresses other gatekeepers (e.g. selection panel members). Thus, linguistically speaking, local knowledge gets at best glossed over or rendered exotic, at worst it gets almost fully marginalized (Boussebaa & Tienari, 2019). Furthermore, over time and in line with the increasing homogenization of knowledge, there is also a shift in the epistemic knowledge base in the field (Ibarra-Colado, 2006) in so far as critical and local perspectives become the unpublishable as they represent the 'uninteresting other'.

Conclusion: language speaks us

In an ironic challenge to the beginning of this chapter, where it was stated that the sentence 'shade provides the tree' cannot be written without its grammatical falseness and general nonsensical nature being noticed, it shall now be stated that 'language speaks us' – more so than we speak language. This dare to the conventional grammatical order plays on the notion that language shapes our perspective about the ordering of the social world, and it does so mainly unbeknown to ourselves. In this regard, the English language speaks the knowledge available and yet to be created of management and business studies. It does so in such a way that its in-built logic and views strongly shape the knowledge creating work in this field. Critics have referred to mental colonialism, or cultural and indeed linguistic imperialism and that minds need to be decolonized. Linguistic professor Wierzbicka (2014) writes about how and why whole academic fields are 'imprisoned by English', where English is used in an absolute way as the only tool through which the world can be labelled and understood. Becoming aware of such mental occupation is the first step of developing practices that continue to challenge its dominance (see Chapter 5 in particular).

References

Agar, M. (1994). *Language shock. Understanding the culture of conversation.* New York: William Morrow and Company.

Akkerman, D., Harzing A. W. and van Witteloostuija, A. (2010). Cultural accommodation and language priming. Competitive versus cooperative behavior in a prisoner's dilemma game. *Management International Review*, 50, 559–583.

Boussebaa, M. and Brown, A. (2017). Englishization, identity regulation and imperialism, *Organization Studies*, 38, 1, 7–29.

Boussebaa, M. and Tienari, J. (2019). Englishization and the politics of knowledge production in management studies. *Journal of Management Inquiry*, doi.org//10.1177/1056492619835.

Canagarajah, A. S. (1996). 'Non-discursive requirements in academic publishing, material resources of periphery scholars, and the politics of knowledge production. *Written Communication*, 13, 4, 435–472.

Chidlow, A., Plakoyiannaki, E. and Welch, C. (2014). Translation in cross-language international business research: Beyond equivalence. *Journal of International Business Studies*, 45, 562–582.

Crystal, D. (2002). *The Cambridge encyclopaedia of language*. Cambridge: Cambridge University Press.

Crystal, D. (2003). *English as a global language*. 2nd. Ed. Cambridge: Cambridge University Press.

Czarniawska, B. (1999). *Writing management: Organization theory as a literary genre*. Oxford: Oxford University Press.

Duranti, A. (2000). *Linguistic anthropology*, Cambridge: Cambridge University Press.

Ehrenreich, B. (2014). *Living with a wild God: A nonbeliever's search for the truth about everything*. New York: Granta Books Publishing.

Flowerdew, J. (2000). Discourse university, legitimate peripheral participation and the non-native English-speaking scholar, *TESOL Quarterly 34*, 127–150.

Gaggiotti, H. and Marre, D. (2017). The words leader/lider and their resonances in an Italo-Latin American multinational corporation. *Leadership*, 13, 2, 194–214.

Grey, C. (2010). Organizing studies: Publications, politics and polemic, *Organization Studies*, 31, 6, 677–694.

Halliday, R. (2003). Written language, standard language, global language, *World Englishes*, 22, 4, 405–418.

Ibarra-Colado, E. (2006). Organization studies and epistemic coloniality in Latin America: Thinking otherness from the margins. *Organization*, 13, 463–488.

Janssens, M. and Steyaert, C. (2014). Reconsidering language within a cosmopolitan understanding: Toward a multilingual franca approach in international business studies, *Journal of International Business Studies*, 45, 5, 623–639.

Kachru, B. B. (1986). The power ad politics of English, *World Englishes*, 5, 2/2, 121–140.

Lillis, T. and Curry, J. (2014). *Academic writing in a global context: The politics and practices of publishing in English*. London: Taylor and Francis.

Ljosland, R. (2007). English in Norwegian academia: A step towards diglossia? *World Englishes*, *26*, 4, 395–410.

Louhiala-Salminen, L., Charles, M. and Kankaanranta, A. (2005). English as lingua franca in Nordic corporate mergers: Two case companies. *English for Specific Purposes*, *24*, 401–421.

Macdonald, S. and Kam, J. (2007). Ring a ring o'roses: Quality journals and gamesmanship in management studies. *Journal of Management Studies*, *44*, 5, 835–845.

Manzella, P. (2019). Culture, language and translation in comparative employee relations: The case of the Italian Caporalato. In K. Koch and P. Manzella (Eds.). *International comparative employee relations. The role of culture and language*, (pp. 106–118). Cheltenham, UK: Edward Elgar.

Meriläinen, A., Tienari, J., Thomas, R. and Davies, A. (2008). Hegemonic academic practices: Experiences of publishing from the periphery. *Organization*, *15*, 4, 584–597.

Montgomery, S. L. (2013). *Does science need a global language English and the future of research*. Chicago and London: University of Chicago Press.

Ostler, N. (2005). *Empires of the word: A language history of the world*. London: HarperCollins Publishers.

Ostler, N. (2010). *The last lingua franca: English until the return of Babel*. London: Allen Lane.

Philippson, R. (1992). *Linguistic imperialism*. Oxford: Oxford University Press.

Philippson, R. (2009). Cultures, contexts and world Englishes. *World Englishes*, *28*, 1, 136–138.

Phipps, A. (2019). *Decolonising multilingualism. Struggles to decreate*. Bristol: Multilingual Matters.

Reich, R. (2001). *The future of success*. New York: Alfred A. Kopf.

Sapir, E. (1949). *Selected writings of Edward Sapir in language, culture and personality*. (Ed.). D. G. Mandelbaum, Berkeley, Los Angeles: University of California Press.

Schedliztki, D., Ahonen, P., Edwards, G. and Gaggiotti, H. (2016). Working with language: A refocused research agenda for cultural leadership studies. International Journal of *Management Reviews*, *19*, 2, 237–257.

Steyaert, C. and Janssens, M. (2013). Multilingual scholarship and the paradox of translation and language in management and organization studies. *Organization*, *20*, 1, 131–142.

Thomas, R., Tienari, J., Davies, A. and Meriläinen, S. (2009). Let's talk about "us": A reflexive account of a cross-cultural research collaboration. *Journal of Management Inquiry*, *18*, 4, 313–324.

Tietze, S. (2009). The work of management academics: An English language perspective, *English for Specific Purposes*, *2*, 371–386.

Tietze, S. (2018). Multilingual research, monolingual publications: Management scholarship in English only? *European Journal of International Management*, *12*, 1–2, 28–45.

Tietze, S. and Dick, P. (2013). The victorious English language: Hegemonic practices in the management academy. *Journal of Management Inquiry, 22,* 1, 122–134.

Üsdiken, B. (2010). Between contending perspectives and logics: Organizational studies in Europe, *Organization Studies, 31,* 6, 715–735.

Vandermeeren, S. (1999). English as lingua franca in written corporate communication: Findings from a European survey. In F. Bargiela-Chiappinie and C. Nickerson (Eds.). *Writing business: Genres, media and discourses,* 273–291, Harlow: Pearson.

Wierzbicka, A. (2014). *Imprisoned in English: The hazards of English as a default language.* Oxford: Oxford University Press.

3 English, language diversity and translation in management research

George Steiner, the eminent translation scholar, proposes that translation is the fundamental mechanism of all human communication in so far as it is always based on efforts to create meaning and understanding:

> Translation, that harvest of Babel, is indeed of the essence. (...) Every act and motion of meaning comports translation. (...) The receiver 'translates', has to translate what he [sic] hears, reads or perceives. Pre-eminently, he does so within his [sic] own tongue, Translation is, first and foremost, intralingual.
>
> (Steiner, 1997, p. 97)

Translation has been embraced by management and organization studies in different ways and in this chapter some approaches will be introduced. The selected studies for this chapter do not present a full review of available thinking, studies or approaches, rather the focus is on establishing their take on language, communication and consequently on translation.

It is also important to note that translation carries different meanings within the different schools of thoughts that will be introduced. For example, within Scandinavian Institutionalism, translation is used to capture the notion of movement of ideas, practices, objects and so forth as they travel across the globe and is received and adopted to local traditions and practices. Within glocalization literature, translation is seen as the process that aligns the global with the local. Organizational change literature uses translation in a broad sense, almost synonymous with change in itself. Some attempts to provide a more grained taxonomy of translation within this literature are also introduced in this chapter. What unites these different takes on translation is that they all espouse translation in the sense captured by George Steiner in the opening quote of this chapter.

The great translation scholar George Steiner offers an understanding of translation as an ongoing act of meaning making, which is the very basis for human communication. Translation is within the above quote described as *intralingual*, i.e. it is about the acts of meaning making that are activated within every communication as incoming signs, symbols, acts, behaviours and words need to be made sense of, i.e. translated in such a way to enable the receiver of the incoming messages to understand and also to respond to them. This broad understanding of translation informs several schools of thoughts within business and management studies. In the second part of this chapter, a body of work is introduced which concerns itself more strongly with language diversity and henceforth also with *interlingual* translation, i.e. translation of meanings between different languages. The main argument within this chapter is that both forms of translation, i.e. intralingual and interlingual, are important in multilingual organizational settings, where both are ongoing and unfolding, rather than being concrete and defined communication spaces.

The chapter ends by commenting on some quite recent studies, which have begun to align these different schools of thoughts and their respective positions about the relationship between words and worlds: Recent empirical and conceptual pieces that use both intra-and interlingual translation to research organizational settings are introduced.

The sources that will be introduced share a common denominator about the relationship between words and worlds: They espouse constructionist epistemologies, that is to say they view language as used in contexts and the relationship between words (language) and the world (context) is considered to be a mutually constitutive one. This is not to say that there was no prior research on the role of language plurality within international business, in particular preceding the contemporary development (Brannen & Mughan, 2017). However, early studies focused more strongly on methodological considerations in cross-national research and cross-cultural management rather than on the significance of language plurality for the strategy and inner workings of the multinational corporation (e.g. Luo & Shenkar, 2006).

An important contribution was made by a school of thought located within organization studies, known as *Communication as Constitutive of Organization* (CCO), which provides the foundations of a constructionist perspective on the use of communications in their form and shapes (e.g. as dialogue, conversation, metaphor, discourse). It includes organizational *change literature*, where translation is seen as expressive and constitutive of *organizational* transformation, or indeed as being opposed to it. *Scandinavian Institutionalism* thinking is strongly based on the framing of the world of business and management as being 'on the move', where knowledge/ideas are uprooted and travel around sectors, industries and indeed also around the globe. Translation understood as change through movement is a key concept of this school of thought. A related way of thinking about global processes is derived from academics who talk about *Glocalization*, where the local and the global are seen in a mutually constitutive relationship.

In contrast, a body of work labelled language-sensitive international business (Piekkari & Tietze, 2011, p. 267) shares an interest in language, but provides a perspective that is quite different from other literatures as its inquiry focus on the existence and relationship of several languages within multilingual settings and how these relationships are constitutive of organizational order and also change thereof. Most recently, this academic community has turned to translation to understand the constitution of multilingual organizations through language plurality. Yet, this take on translation is interlingual, i.e. concerned with the occurrence of translation activity from source to target language in situ, i.e. as found within ongoing organizational (multilingual) communications. It thus uses interlingual translation as a means to unpack the constitutions of multilingual organizations.

Communication as Constitutive of Organization (CCO)

This scholarship asks a central question, that is how organizations happen in and through communication – rather than imagining organizations as containers in which communications happen. This question has become central for scholars who view organizations as constituted through communication, which includes acts such as the activation of discourses, stories, narratives and metaphorical framing. Schoeneborn, Kuhn and Kärreman (2019) take ontological umbrage with a view of language that still treats it as a system of reference for denoting objects – which they contrast with a take on language that sees meaning based on what users 'assign to language to distinguish certain experiences from one another' (p. 478). This analysis takes language-based research deeply into questions of how and why meaning is generated and why it can be so unstable and varied, and why the relationships between words and the world are inherently indeterminate and conflict-laden. Language is seen to 'constitute the world, yes, but as a result of struggle and negotiation and not by mechanistic determination' (p. 478).

The literature has developed quite a rich understanding of how language (communication) and discourse unfold, including which forms and outlets they take, whether and how they can be disruptive, generative, conservative, or creative and progressive (Schoeneborn *et al.*, 2019). The importance of this language/communication-based framing of organizations cannot be underestimated as this has enabled generations of researchers to see organizations and organizational phenomena as coming into being, persisting and being transformed through interconnected communication practices (Ashcraft, Kuhn & Cooren, 2009; Cooren, Taylor & van Every, 2006).

Translation as organizational change

Of particular interest here is, however, the use of translation within the organizational change literature, which is in line with CCO thinking that sees change as enabled, carried and constituted through the activation and ongoing unfolding of discourse and meaning systems. Within this thinking, there is some evidence that translation has been drawn upon as a conceptual tool to understand the (micro)dynamics of unfolding change within organizational settings.

A particular contribution by Doolin, Grant and Thomas (2013) understands organizational change 'as arising from, and comprising, ongoing, iterative, and recursive process of translation' (Doolin *et al.*, 2013, p. 253), through which new meanings are introduced and taken up within organizations. Translation is understood 'to be the modifying, adjusting, and changing of specific change initiatives by particular actors in context in relation to their particular agendas' (p. 253).

Within the editorial article by Doolin *et al.* (2013), they develop a categorization of the function of translation within different change scenarios: *Translation as engagement* sees organizations as conversationally constructed realities and organizational change is seen to be achieved by change agents to facilitate a change in the conversations. Translation is part of changing organizational conversations. Dialogue becomes a means of co-constructing meanings between organizational members. *Translation as endless transmutations* is also focusing on the organization as an emerging achievement with conversations being understood as translating meaning in an ongoing manner: 'Translation can be understood as endless transmutations of the organization forms and reforms in communicative interaction' (p. 256).

Yet these ongoing conversational forms of dialogue and meaning change are always accompanied by struggles over meanings and therefore caught up in relations of power. Doolin *et al.* relate to this as *Translation as Struggle*, where different actors bring their perspectives, values and vested interest to the ongoing negotiations and the change process can also be resisted, subverted and appropriated. *Translation as translocation* is concerned with 'the movement of meanings across space and times to bring about institutional change' (p. 257). Translocation approaches stressed that through the translation of new meanings across institutional, meanings are not merely spread, but that they are actively reshaped as they move across time and space. It can be brought to bear on understanding the use of translation within Scandinavian Institutionalism, which is discussed in the next section. *Translation as transgression* can be seen as related to the 'translation as struggle' approach as it acknowledges translation as a way through which resistance to change can be expressed and enacted.

Translation as transgression focuses on the exploration of 'other voices' (p. 259) in the change process, e.g. the voices of subordinates or the voices of managers in translating change initiatives for their own interests and the means they deploy to do so. The last approach is titled *Translation as Colonization* and the authors turn to the production of knowledge about organizations and the use of language (English) in the research process, pointing to issues of privileging the English language scholarship – a theme that is central to this book and explored across several chapters.

Scandinavian Institutionalism and Glocalization

Scandinavian Institutionalism is a school of thought that asks questions of how and why ideas, practices and objects change when they start to travel across sectors, industries or national-institutional-cultural boundaries (Czarniawska & Sevón, 1996, 2005). It also embraces the notion of 'the global' in so far as it questions why and how a practice changes sometimes so drastically when it leaves its place of origin and is received 'elsewhere'. Scandinavian Institutionalism centres on a specific definition of translation as 'the modification that a practice or an idea undergoes when it is implemented in a new organizational context' (Boxenbaum & Strandgaard Pedersen, 2009, pp. 190–191).

The transformation of practice is treated as agentic, i.e. it is in the 'hand of the people; each of which may act in different ways, letting the token drop, or modifying it, or deflecting it, or betraying it; or adding to it, or appropriating it' (Latour, 1986, p. 267). The receivers of incoming practices or ideas are not seen as passive adopters, but as active editors (Sahlin & Wedlin, 2008) that are embedded, yet empowered, actors who can channel and shape new practices. These local actors are the very editors and comprise a wide array of roles including organizational ones such as leaders or local managers as well as external ones such as academics, consultants or experts. They are then indeed like metaphorical translators and active change agents who can influence local interpretation and whose interest and motives also influence the reception process – with the twist being that in multilingual settings their editing work has a lot to do with interlingual translation as will be shown later in this chapter. *Scandinavian Institutionalism*, on the whole, does not concern itself with interlingual translation, because the espoused take on translation is far reaching and manifold and therefore surpasses the linguistic interpretation (Czarniawska & Joerges, 1996, p. 24).

Similarly, a body of work sometimes labelled as *Glocalization* focuses on the transformational process that occurs when the global and the local meet. It sees the global and the local in a mutually constitutive relationship, hence the word glocal. Within the glocal encounter, complexities unfold and are recognized as the '"what", "who" and "how"' through which the dualities of 'similarity and variation as well as universalism and parochialism' (Drori, Höllerer & Walgenbach, 2014, p. 85) are made.

Just like the literatures briefly introduced above, its take on culture and language are non-essentialist, that is to say they are constitutive processes in which meaning is seen to cross national-cultural boundaries; Meyer (2014, p. 81) points to the 'overcoming of meaning boundaries' in so far as

> meaningful items cannot be transported 'wholesale' from one cultural context to another ... They have to pass through a powerful filter of local cultural and structural constraints to also gain legitimacy in their new local context and can, thus, only spread if they resonate within this context.

Micro-mobilizations of discursive tools are employed to enable the glocal encounter. These micro-strategies are language-based, i.e. discursive enactments of the glocal process. For example, Boxenbaum and Gond (2014, p. 316) identify several such discursive micro-strategies of contextualization, filtering, reframing and bricolage. These include the changes in the construct in question (responsible investment), its discursive realignment with local history and current trends, and its integration into existing practices. It is possible to understand these agentic processes as similar to editorial activity developed within *Scandinavian Institutionalism*. Some glocalization scholars alike the local agents to 'glocalizers' who marshal discursive resources to influence the fusion process of the global and the local across time and space (Drori *et al.*, 2014, p. 92) and which are 'positioned at the junctions of translation'

(Drori *et al.*, 2014, p. 92) and are therefore the most likely of the (local) agents who can overcome the meaning boundaries concomitant to glocal processes. It stands to reason that such interstices are multilingual and the global arrives often in and through the English language and meets with the local language/s. If this is so, and research to be discussed in the next part provides plenty of evidence that this is indeed the case, then the local agents are editors, metaphorical translators (i.e. sense-givers) and also interlingual translators.

Before proceeding to introducing a body of literature that has developed a quite different understanding of language and its use in organizational settings, it is beneficial to summarize the contribution of the above approaches to our understanding of translation. This understanding is based on Steiner's notion of intralingual translation, i.e. the meaning-making processes that underpin every communicative encounter within the same language. Here, CCO approaches stress the ongoing, constitutive nature of such encounters and relating this to translation, it becomes a continuous unfolding of meaning making in complex settings and it can be seen as being the essence of organizational change. Scandinavian Institutionalism explicitly links translation to movement and change, where transformation is seen to be an agentic process of meaning making in the light of something 'new' arriving. Glocalization has contributed to the notion of the glocal, and translators are seen to be positioned in powerful positions at the interstices where the global and the local meet.

Language-sensitive research in international management

In the past three decades a stream of studies has gelled into what was labelled in 2011 by Piekkarie and Tietze (2011, p. 267) as language-sensitive international business research and is referred to today more broadly as language-based international management research. Over time it has developed into an identifiable field of inquiry that seeks to understand the processes, institutional agents and consequences of cross-border, cross-language organization and management. There are to date three academic reviews of this literature. Karhunen, Kankaanranta, Louhiala-Salminen and Piekkari (2018) who unearth the assumptions found in articles within language-sensitive research in international management as structural, functional or social practice perspectives, i.e. with the social practice view being identified as the most promising for future inquiry.

Tenzer, Terjesen and Harzing (2017) focus on language diversity in multinational corporations and summarize core findings by individual, group, firm and country levels of analysis. Future research agendas based on the transcendence of disciplinary boundaries and integrating with other disciplinary fields are identified. Tietze and Piekkari (2020) provide a historical reading of the development of this particular field of inquiry and differentiate between three junctures (late 1980s to 2010 where languages were much treated as a sideshow in research mainly within multinational corporations; 2011–2014 where the field began to form and gathered momentum; and from 2015 onwards where calls for deeper philosophical debates and methodological approaches aligned with calls for integration with other business, organization and management fields of inquiry). These authors point to the notion of interlingual translation as an emerging key concept within this field and, together with English, the second (yet mainly ignored) means of global communication.

The pertinent themes of this field of inquiry are to an extent different from the discursive interests of other literatures. Investigations into the role and use of English as a dominant language in international business marked the field's intellectual direction to a large extent. However, with such inquiry comes related questions such as what are then the role and use of 'other' languages and how do they relate to English.

In this regard this community has established the use of 'English' as a legitimate topic for research – and by extension also the topic of language diversity. Language in this field is understood as in the English, the German, the Finnish, the Chinese language and so on; the broad focus of inquiry is to understand the relationship between English and other languages. Empirical studies, for example, discuss (mainly) English and its use as a Common Corporate Language and how this shapes individual and collective relationships with non-native English speakers or amongst speakers of different languages (e.g. Vaara, Tienari, Piekkari & Säntti, 2005); how it is used in different organizational stages, e.g. back stage and front stage; how it plays out in adoption and contestations between Business English as a lingua franca (BELF) and English as a lingua franca (ELF) and native speaker or elite speaker usage (Louhiala-Salminen, Charles & Kankaanranta, 2005); how it remains contested (Gabrois & Nentwich, 2020; Lønsman, 2017) and how its adoption as a corporate language creates as many problems as it allegedly addresses (Sanden & Kankaanranta, 2019) and destabilizes some other working language practices (Langinier & Ehrhart, 2019). Scholars within this tradition use terms such as language diversity, multilingualism and *linguascaping* (Steyeart, Ostendorp & Gabrois, 2011) to capture the relational, political and contextual factors that shape language use in multilingual settings. The literature also acknowledges that English is not a monolithic phenomenon, but is varied, multifaceted, complex and how it is used is adding layers of additional complexities within multilingual organizations.

The field debunked the myth that organizations will ever be monolingual and much of its intellectual energy flows into establishing the multifaceted phenomena that constitute and express such entangled diversity (Brannen, Piekkari & Tietze, 2014). One such phenomenon is the occurrence of translation work because the experiences of researching those working in multilingual settings revealed that interim, fragmented, spontaneous, unregulated translation work is an ongoing – if so, far mainly ignored – phenomena of multilingual work settings (Piekkari, Tietze & Koskinen, 2020).

Translation

In terms of language-sensitive research within international management and organization, there are studies that document translation as it unfolds in situ (Piekkari, Welch, Welch, Peltonen & Vesa, 2013) in multilingual organizational settings. Invariably, it is shown to be agentic, dispersed, varied, incomplete, difficult to achieve, contested and situated within historical-political contexts as much as it is driven by business expediencies (Logemann & Piekkari, 2015; Ciuk & James, 2015; Kettunen, 2016; Ciuk, James & Śliwa, 2019; Treguer-Felten, 2017; Tietze, Tansley & Helienek, 2017). It is also shown to be done by *paraprofessional translators*, who engage in interlingual translation as part of their daily work, but are not trained translators or interpreters (Koskela, Koskinen & Pilke, 2017; Tuylenev, 2014), i.e. they are glocalizers and editors identified in other literatures as organizational or institutional agents who perform institutional linking (or refuse to do so or do so only partially) through their interlingual translation work (Tietze *et al.*, 2017).

These paraprofessional translators (and interpreters) are normal employees like office workers, team leaders or managers who have competence in more than one language. Their formal work remit does not include translation work; yet due to the expedience of working in a multilingual environment, they have to activate their translation abilities. They have been shown to be highly active, influential agents who have often considerable agency to shape incoming texts, meanings and practices in line with their own or the localities preferences.

Empirical studies within the language-sensitive international management literature are concerned with documenting, tracking and analysing the role of *interlingual translation* in knowledge transfer and decision making (Logemann & Piekkari, 2015), as part of micro-political manoeuvring (Piekkari & Tietze, 2014). Their use of interlingual translation becomes possible as English is not taken as a universal language and language plurality as experienced in the researched settings requires many different language-based practices (see Steyaert, Ostendorp & Gabrois, 2011; Janssens & Steyaert, 2014), including interlingual translation. From thereon, interlingual translation has become a focus of interest and a topic worthy of investigation. Westney and Piekkari's (2020) paper is an example of how to draw on the tradition of *Scandinavian Institutionalism* and its understanding of translation while also incorporating interlingual translation thinking into their historical analysis of the movement of organizational practices from Japan to the US. The authors then develop a precise and theoretically based categorization of the elements of *translation ecology* that includes translators, translations and translation processes.

The community of language sensitive scholars has generated an impressive amount of empirical studies of different research philosophies and thematic priorities (see in particular Tenzer *et al.* (2017) for some detailed composite analysis of the literature). Important conceptual impetus has been provided by some papers. Janssens, Lambert and Steyaert (2004) write about language strategies within international business companies from a translation perspective and differentiated between mechanistic, cultural and political models of translation. Holden (2008) and Holden and Michailova (2014) articulate the complexities of translating the discourses of knowledge management from English into other languages, i.e. Russian. Chidlow, Plakoyiannaki and Welch (2014) problematize the lack of and at best constrained use of interlingual translation within international business research and theorized their findings in terms of the dominance of an equivalence paradigm.

Most recently, Piekkari *et al.* (2020) have written about the nexus of ties between metaphorical (i.e. intralingual) and interlingual translation in multilingual settings. They base their arguments on a matrix of the two forms of translation, i.e. metaphorical (intralingual, sense-making and sense-giving) and interlingual, and show them to be in a mutually constitutive relationship. In doing so, they attempt to bring interlingual translation more strongly into organization and management studies and to break its (relative) isolation as a topic of research only relevant within a subfield of international business. Koskinen (2020), a translation studies professor, who is also conducting research in multilingual work places, proposes to conceptualize multilingual organizations as *spaces of translation*.

Leaning on Cronin (2006, p. 68) multilingual organizations are seen as spaces where translation needs to happen for mutual comprehensibility and where multilingual practices meet and mix. Translation is not to be seen as the tasks of translation departments in the production of final texts or the outsourcing of such work to translation agencies, but as ongoing and a widespread practice, fluid and porous and including orality and *translatorialtiy*, i.e. the constant movement between languages and meaning. From thereon Koskinen proposes to conceptualize multilingual work organization as *translatorial spaces*.

Recent developments within translation-sensitive international management research

There exist by now a handful of empirical studies that document the intense and difficult work done by paraprofessional translators. Kettunen (2016) demonstrates how interlingual translation is central to the travel and reception of International Financial Reporting Standards and that it can be theorized as a central to the doing of institutional work. Transporting (English) reporting standards into Finnish language environments requires ongoing and laboursome engagement of multiple and changing constituencies into the interlingual translation process before such standards can become more deeply accepted and embedded.

Thus, Kettunen shows interlingual translation as central to complex, ongoing and contested institutional interactions in support of transnational regulations. The contribution of this chapter is quite exceptional: It clearly shows the ongoing, central and dispersed collective character of (interlingual) translation and theorizes these ongoing acts of interlingual translation through one of the main concepts of organizational institutionalism, i.e. institutional work. It is set within a key functional area of business, i.e. auditing and accounting, and therefore it demonstrates how relevant interlingual translation can be to research the processes of transnational knowledge transfer.

Ciuk *et al.* (2019) and Ciuk and James (2015) show how interlingual translation can be deliberately used as a management tool to advance desired behaviour within a subsidiary unit within a US Headquarter – Polish subsidiary structure: Interlingual translation decisions provide the space for the unfolding of micro-political and power-based practices and relationships, paving the way for the reception of the US/English-language change programme. The effects or consequences of interlingual translation decisions are described as 'purposing', 'reframing', 'domesticating' and 'inscribing' – in other words interlingual translation decisions are constitutive of how the incoming practices are received and consequently enacted.

Interlingual translation is then a discursive resource not unlike other discursive resources established in related literatures, e.g. the reframing achieved through using particular discursive devices as identified within the glocalization literature by Boxenbaum and Gond (2014) or the discursive devices underpinning the translation of management ideas identified by Mueller and Whittle (2011) within Scandinavian Institutionalism or the discursive approaches identified by Doolin *et al.* (2013) underpinning change processes or the 'funnelling of interests' through translation in periods of organizational change (Whittle, Suhomlinova & Mueller, 2010).

Conclusion

In this chapter some literatures that have either made translation central to their project (e.g. Scandinavian Institutionalism) or have drawn upon it to clarify some of their own key constructs (e.g. the change construct within organizational change literature) or as a means to understand the hybrid outcomes of glocal encounters have been introduced. These briefly introduced literatures are all based on constructionist epistemologies, where the word and the world are seen in a mutually constitutive relationship. Translation is seen as mainly agentic and transformative.

As a point of critique and despite the significance of the contributions made by these connected literatures, they share a common denominator in that they are almost completely *monolingual* at the very latest at the stage of publication, i.e. of knowledge dissemination. 'Other languages' may not exist as well. English is treated (unconsciously one assumes) as the universal language of management knowledge (Tietze, 2018). Logically, from thereon there is no need for translation or it is treated as an administrative-mechanistic necessity: The literature is monolingually English and interlingually translation-blind: Meanings of words, meanings of the world and meanings of practices are already and always present and fully recognizable in English.

There is no other language that would merit any form of representation within these accounts or that would merit further analysis. Omission, however, is always a political act and in this regard the lack of representation of the 'language other' symbolizes not only a lack of interest in it or an ill-informed disregard of its importance, but it can be seen as expressive of the privileging of English as the language of the (academic) elite. English is treated as synonymous with its status of the taken-for-granted language of progress, prosperity and success.

In contrast, the language-sensitive international management literature has made English and its relationship to other languages a central
theme of its project – and it has begun to turn to (interlingual) translation, understood as a language practice through which multilingual
organizations are constituted. It has not as yet, though, fully explored
the rich potential of integrating the insights gained from the intra-
translatorially inspired literature. In this regard its contribution to central themes of organization and management studies (i.e. how and why
does organizational change occur; how can one explain the phenomena
of institutional coupling, for example, from a language and interlingual
translation perspective) is yet to be discovered and explored within this
literature.

In taking the language project forward, it will be discussed how to
integrate the insights from these diverse literatures with a view to present a more elaborate perspective in language and translation as they
unfold and are used in organizational settings. In 2003, Deetz claimed
that the legacy of the linguistic turn in organization and management
studies is yet to be achieved as more than just turning attention to language, it points rather to its constitutive ability. Alvesson and Kärreman
(2000) talked about the linguistic turn in terms of discourse and
Discourse. The former small 'd' discourse is based on individuals or collective using available meaning resources to talk about themselves and
their positions – an example would be how one talks about one's career.
The big 'D' discourse is the framing aspects of such talk, and Alvesson
and Kärreman use the example of how management consultants talk
about careers in terms of two overarching big Discourses: Ambition
and Autonomy.

From the perspective of this book, however, the linguistic turn will
not be complete unless it includes considerations that within multilingual settings, discourse and Discourse are packed into language and
languages not as a mere 'vehicle of meaning' but as an active agentic-
creative aspect of meaning making. Thus, language diversity and
English are part and parcel of the constitutive process of the multilingual organization, be it as Discourse or as discourse.

References

Alvesson, M. and Kärreman, D. (2000). Taking the linguistic turn in organiza-
tional research. *Journal of Applied Behavioral Science, 36*, 136–158.
Ashcraft, K. L., Kuhn, T. R. and Cooren, F. (2009). Constitutional amendments.
"Materializing" organizational communication. *Academy of Management
Annals, 3*, 1, 1–64.

Boxenbaum, E. and Gond, J. P. (2014). Micro-strategies of contextualization: Glocalizing responsible investment in France and Quebec. In G. S. Drori, M. A. Höllerer and P. Walgenbach (Eds.). *Global themes and local variations in organization and management*, (pp. 311–324). Abingdon: Routledge.

Boxenbaum, E. and Strandgaard Pedersen, J. (2009). Scandinavian institutionalism: A case of institutional work. In T. B. Lawrence, R. Suddaby, and B. Leca (Eds.). *Institutional work: Actors and agency in institutional studies of organization*, (pp. 178–204). Cambridge, UK: Cambridge University Press.

Brannen, M. Y. and Mughan, T. (2017). *Language in international business: Developing a field*. Basingstoke: Palgrave Macmillan.

Brannen, M. Y., Piekkari, R. and Tietze, S. (2014). The multifaceted role of language in international business: Unpacking the forms, functions and features of a critical challenge to MNC theory and performance. *Journal of International Business Studies 45*, 5, 495–507.

Chidlow, A., Plakoyiannaki, E. and Welch, C. (2014). Translation in cross-language international business research: Beyond equivalence. *Journal of International Business Studies, 45*, 562–582.

Ciuk, S. and James, P. (2015). Interlingual translation and transfer of value-infused practices: An in-depth qualitative exploration. *Management Learning, 46*, 565–581.

Ciuk, S., James, P. and Śliwa, M. (2019). Micropolitical dynamics of interlingual translation processes in an MNC subsidiary. *British Journal of Management. 30*, 4, 926–942. Retrieved from https://doi.org/10.1111/1467-8551.12323.

Cooren, F., Taylor, J. R. and van Every, E. J. (2006). *Communication as organizing. Empirical and theoretical explorations in the dynamic of text and conversation*. Mahwah, NJ: Lawrence Erlbaum Associates.

Cronin, M. (2006). *Translation and identity*. London and New York: Routledge.

Czarniawska, B. and Joerges, B. (1996). *Translating organizational change*, (pp. 13–48). Berlin, Germany: de Gruyter.

Czarniawska, B. and Sevón, G. (1996). *Translating organizational change*. Berlin, Germany: de Gruyter.

Czarniawska, B. and Sevón, G. (2005). *Global ideas: How ideas, objects and practices travel in the global economy*. Copenhagen, Denmark: Liber & Copenhagen Business School Press.

Deetz, S. A. (2003). Reclaiming the legacy of the linguistic turn, *Organization, 10*, 421–429.

Doolin, B., Grant, D. and Thomas, R. (2013). Translating translation and change: Discourse-based approaches, *Journal of Change Management, 13*, 3, 251–265.

Drori, G. S., Höllerer, M. A. and Walgenbach, P. (2014). *Global themes and local variations in organization and management: Perspectives on glocalization*. New York, NY: Routledge.

Gabrois, C. and Nentwich, J. (2020). The dynamics of privilege: How employees of a multinational corporation construct and contest the privileging effects of English proficiency, *Canadian Journal of Administrative Science, 1*, 1–15.

Holden, N. (2008). German. A language of management designed for Klarheit. In S. Tietze (Ed.). *International management and language*, (pp. 14–127). Abingdon: Routledge.

Holden, N. J. and Michailova, S. (2014). A more expansive perspective on translation in IB research: Insights from the Russian handbook of knowledge management, *Journal of International Business Studies 45*, 7, 906–918.

Janssens, M. and Steyaert, C. (2014). Reconsidering language within a cosmopolitan understanding: Toward a multilingual franca approach in international business studies, *Journal of International Business Studies, 45*, 5, 623–639.

Janssens, M., Lambert, J. and Steyaert, C. (2004). Developing language strategies for international companies: The contribution of translation studies, *Journal of World Business 39*, 4, 414–430.

Karhunen, P., Kankaanranta, A., Louhiala-Salminen, L. and Piekkari, R. (2018). Let's talk about language: A review of language-sensitive research in international management, *Journal of Management Studies, 55*, 6, 980–1013.

Kettunen, J. (2016). Interlingual translation of the International Financial Reporting Standards as institutional work, *Accounting, Organizations and Society, 56*, 38–54.

Koskela, M., Koskinen, K. and Pilke, N. (2017). Bilingual formal meeting as a context of translatoriality, *Target, 29,* 464–485.

Koskinen, K. (2020). Translatorial linguistic ethnography in organizations. In S. Horn, P. Lecomte and S. Tietze (Eds.). *Managing the multilingual workplace: Methodological, empirical and pedagogic perspectives*, 60–78. Abingdon: Routledge.

Langinier, H. and Ehrhard, S. (2019). When local meets global: How introducing English destabilizes translanguaging practices in a cross-border organization, *Management International, 1*, 1–14.

Latour, B. (1986). The powers of association. In J. Law (Ed.). *Power, action and belief: A new sociology of knowledge?* London, UK: Routledge and Kegan Paul.

Logemann, M. and Piekkari, R. (2015). 'Localise or local lies?' The power of language and translation in the multinational corporation, *Critical Perspectives on International Business, 11*, 30–53.

Lønsman, D. (2017). Embrace it or resist it? Employees' reception of corporate language policies, *International Journal of Cross Cultural Management, 17*, 1, 101–124.

Louhiala-Salminen, L., Charles, M. and Kankaanranta, A. (2005). English as lingua franca in Nordic corporate mergers: Two case companies, *English for Specific Purposes, 24*, 401–421.

Luo, Y. and Shenkar. O. (2006). The multinational corporation as a multilingual community: Language and organization in a global context *Journal of International Business Studies 37*, 3, 321–339.

Meyer, R. E. (2014). Re-localization as micro-mobilization of consent and legitimacy. In G. S. Drori, M. A. Höllerer, and P. Walgenbach (Eds.). *Global themes and local variations in organization and management: Perspectives on glocalization*, (pp. 79–89). New York, NY: Routledge.

Mueller, F. and Whittle, A. (2011). Translating management ideas: A discursive devices analysis. *Organization Studies*, *32*, 2, 187–210.

Piekkari, R. and Tietze, S. (2011). A world of languages: Implications for international management research and practice, *Journal of World Business*. *46*, 3, 267–269.

Piekkari, R. and Tietze, S. (2014). Micropolitical behavior in the multinational enterprise: A language perspective". In Alain Verbeke, Robert Van Tulder, and Sarianna Lundan (Eds.). *Multinational enterprises, markets and institutional Diversity: Progress in international business*, (pp. 259–277). Bingley: Emerald.

Piekkari, R., Tietze, S. and Koskinen, K. (2020). Metaphorical and interlingual translation in moving organizational practices across languages. *Organization Studies*, *41*, 9, 1311–1332.

Piekkari, R., Welch, D. E., Welch, L. S., Peltonen, J. P. and Vesa, T. (2013). Translation behaviour: An exploratory study within a service multinational, *International Business Review*, *22*, 5, 771–783.

Sahlin, K. and Wedlin, L. (2008). Circulating ideas: Imitation, translation and editing. In R. Greenwood, C. Oliver, R. Suddaby and K. Sahlin (Eds.). *The SAGE handbook of organizational institutionalism*, (pp. 218–242). London: Sage.

Sanden, G. R. and Kankaanranta, A. (2019). "English is an unwritten rule here". Non-formalised language policies in multinational corporations, *Corporate Communications: An International Journal*, *23*, 4, 544–566. doi 10.1108/CCIJ-02-2018-0026.

Schoeneborn, D., Kuhn, T. and Kärreman, D. (2019). The communicative constitution of organization, organizing, and organizationality, *Organization Studies*, *40*, 475–496.

Steiner, G. (1997). *Errata: An examined life*. London: Orion Publishing Group.

Steyaert, C., Ostendorp, A. and Gabrois, C. (2011). Multilingual organizations as 'linguascapes': Negotiating the position of English through discursive practices, *Journal of World Business*, *46*, 270–278.

Tenzer, H., Terjesen, S. and Harzing, A. W. (2017). Language in international business research: A review and agenda for future research, *Management International Review*. *57*, 6, 815–854.

Tietze, S. (2018). Multilingual research, monolingual publications: Management scholarship in English only? *European Journal of International Management*, *12*, 28–45.

Tietze, S. and Piekkari. R. (2020.) Languages and cross-cultural management. In Betina Szkudlarek, Joyce S. Osland, Dan V. Caprar, and Laurence Romani (Eds.). *SAGE handbook of contemporary cross-cultural management*, (pp. 181–195). Thousand Oaks, CA: Sage.

Tietze, S., Tansley, C. and Helienek, E. (2017). The translator as agent in talent management knowledge transfer, *International Journal of Cross Cultural Management*, *17*, 151–169.

Treguer-Felten, G. (2017). The role of translation in the cross-cultural transferability of corporate codes of conduct. *International Journal of Cross Cultural Management, 17*, 1, 137–150.

Tuylenev, S. (2014). *Translation and society: An introduction.* London, UK and New York, NY: Routledge.

Vaara, E., Tienari, J., Piekkari, R. and Säntti, R. (2005). Language and the circuits of power in merging multinational organizations, *Journal of Management Studies, 2*, 3, 595–623.

Westney, D. E, and Piekkari. R. (2020). Reversing the translation flow: Moving organizational practices from Japan to the U.S., *Journal of Management Studies, 57*, 1, 57–86.

Whittle, A., Suhomlinova, O. and Mueller, F. (2010). Funnel of interests: The discursive translation of organizational change. *The Journal of Applied Behavioral Science, 46*, 16–37.

4 Towards a reconfiguration of language diversity and translation in management research

Translation is inevitable in cross-language research – despite the existence of English as the (dominant) language of business and management, which oftentimes glosses over the translation work that precedes English language publications. Overall, the field of business and management research has so far failed to establish protocols on how to report such translation work that informs the construction of research accounts. Instead, it is assumed that English is sufficiently universal to express all possible meanings in all possible situated contexts and theoretical perspectives. The novelist Derek B. Miller describes such naïve assumptions about communication, knowledge and translation by pointing to the unaware stance of one of the characters in the novel *The Girl in Green*: 'From here on he [the translator] became Märta's voice, and, like every other Westerner trying to change the world through translators, Märta had no idea what he was actually saying' (Miller, 2016, p. 57).

In this chapter an argument is made that the unreflective use of English in the overall research process within management research has a series of consequences: Consequences pertaining to the representation and analysis of empirical data; for epistemological-philosophical positions; for conceptual-theoretical work and also for the well-being and knowledge contributions of knowledge workers themselves.

These will be discussed by drawing on some 'scattered' studies that have addressed aspects of these themes. The thoughts developed in this chapter align with some aspects of the call by Westwood and Jack (2007) and Westwood (2006) to embrace critical and postcolonial theory and positions and, consequently, to develop different dispositions towards the production of management knowledge. The radical reconfiguration they call for across all aspects of knowledge production, dissemination and practice will be articulated in this chapter, albeit from a language diversity and translation perspective. The main critique of the position advocated by Westwood and Jack is its monolingual orientation – i.e. the criticality and radical reflexivity that they propose does not extend to their own taken-for-grantedness of the English language. Westwood (2006) gets to the core of the issues of working across languages and translating into another language, both in the literal and the metaphorical (cultural) sense.

He, correctly, identifies the inclusion of indigenous locals or researchers as a way to break with colonially informed research practices; however, he, also correctly, points to the pitfalls of such practices which are, amongst others, that they still have to translate their words, practices, experiences and values so that they become receivable and palatable for a Western audience. In other words: 'Indigenous self-representation needs to be a longer-term goal since it would require openness within Western knowledge systems and shifts in the politics of knowledge (for example, radical changes in publishing policies in academic journals' (Westwood, 2006, p. 107). I will return to these issues in the next chapter, where an argument is made that there are at least some inklings that such openness is becoming possible.

Returning to the issues of English language use, as has been shown in previous chapters, there are now research accounts available that clearly and convincingly demonstrate how English and the concomitant subduing or total eradication of translation are in their essence part of (quasi) colonial projects (e.g. Boussebaa & Brown, 2017; Boussebaa & Tiennari, 2019; Tietze, 2004, 2018; Wilmot & Tietze, 2021 forthcoming). These research accounts do present a challenge to the assumptions on which such quasi-colonial thinking is based on; yet to date there is no consolidated body of work to do so, rather the cited pieces remain fragmented.

Critical, postcolonial international management studies

Gavin Jack and Robert Westwood (e.g. Jack, 2004; Jack & Westwood, 2006; Westwood, 2006; Jack, Westwood, Srinivas & Sardar, 2011) have made a significant contribution towards opening a critically interrogative space in which the ongoing effects of colonial projects and their impact on international business and management can be investigated. Postcolonial studies have their origins in literary criticism, but now include cultural studies, translation studies as well as (international) management and organization studies. While theoretical underpinnings vary, it is generally 'concerned with revealing continuities and persistent effects of the colonial project and colonial experience in *contemporary* ways of knowing and acting in the world' (Westwood, 2004, p. 57). It offers a theoretical framework within which the continuing effects of European imperialism and its influence on management can be understood (Mika & O'Sullivan, 2014).

As a political engagement with research practice (Jack & Westwood, 2006), it shows how since the Second World War, centres of management knowledge production have been established primarily within North America and Northern Europe (Jack, 2004; Westwood, 2004, Üsdiken, 2010; Grey, 2010). The two main centres are English-speaking ones – the US and the secondary centre – the UK (Üsdiken, 2010), where management/business thinking, vocabularies and practices were formulated and from where they spread. In terms of research involving peripheral settings or cultures, they become often the cultural. Others are either exoticized or constructed in terms of their opposition to the West, which is depicted as superordinate; and the epitome of modernity and progress, which stood in stark contrast to the more primitive 'Orient' (Said, 1978). From the perspective of management knowledge production, this means that peoples and cultures outside of these dominant centres are frequently essentialized as an object of study (Fougère & Moulettes, 2012) and only 'conceptualised through the refracting lens of Western categories, constructs and theories' (Westwood, 2004, p. 63). The continued dominance of these centres of knowledge production means that its approaches to knowledge production have produced little self-scrutiny and is rarely recognized for the ideologically bound and parochial perspective that it is (Westwood, 2004; Jack, 2004; Jack *et al.*, 2011).

Consequences of monolingual international management research

In their position paper published in 2007, Westwood and Jack examine dominant institutional processes and geopolitical relationships as well as research practices of international business and management studies. From thereon they develop a manifesto for the development of postcolonial theory for international business and management studies. Their principles include epistemological, institutional and methodological considerations with a view to trigger a reconfiguration of the field's understanding and practices of knowledge production. In the context of globalization and evolving forms of imperialism, Westwood (2006, p. 104) writes that it 'creat[ing]es an unbalanced and asymmetrical new world order under western hegemony'.

In terms of the generation and representation of knowledge from a language perspective, a radical rejection of the global language of knowledge and power, English, would make it very difficult, if not impossible to share knowledge at all. This is obviously not the position of this book as its major purpose is to reach a global audience of know-ledge workers, and it needs a shared language to create intelligibility. On the other hand, English is not treated as universally valid construc-tion tool so to speak, but as a linguistic source to be handled with care and awareness. Holland (2002, p. 6) proposes three different positions regarding the treatment of English. One is a sceptical one, in which it is the carrier and means to spread the dominant discursive practices of the Western capitalist discourses around the globe. The second is a neutralist one, whereby English is seen as part of the inevitable process of global change with socio-political causes and effects, but historic-ally there is nothing new bar to the global reach of English. The third position is based on a positive orientation whereby English is seen as a benign discourse that facilitates the export of free, democratic and pluralist modes of economic and political organization. Within these three positions, the nearest to the one within this book is the middle one – however with a stronger emphasis on addressing concomitant malfunctions as encaptured in the sceptical position.

Thus, what is discussed below and taken forward also in Chapter 5 can be described as a project to introduce more hybridity, more foreignness, more disruption, more space for alternative interro-gation into the research process and the written research accounts of international business and management knowledge production. This position aligns with postcolonial positions that offer a counter argument and counter practices to the homogenization and conver-gence entailed in hegemonic processes of knowledge production. Within such thinking local resistance is seen to result in forms and practices of mimicry, hybridity, appropriation and other strategies (Bhabha, 2004).

However, as it is imperative to develop a vocabulary that is steeped in language and translation to unpack these processes, the next section showcases some published pieces that have begun to do so. These are, at this particular contemporary moment, still scattered and individual pieces that are yet to form into a consolidated body of work to address questions of methods and epistemology in the treatment of languages and translation in knowledge production.

Tietze (2018) argues that throughout every step of research (research within multilingual contexts, i.e. what is usually summarized under the descriptors of 'international' or 'comparative'), questions of language and translation arise. In the next section some such steps are discussed from a language and translation perspective.

Outlining and formulating ideas into a project

The early stages of a nascent research project, whether a doctoral one, or a substantive application for research funding, or for writing a book proposal, remain often uncaptured and unexamined. These steps involve a great deal of thinking, words and communications – and may well include taking reference to non-English language resources. Meriläinen, Tienari, Thomas and Davies (2008) and Thomas, Tienari, Davies and Meriläinen (2009) analyse the beginnings of a joint, international (i.e. cross-language) research collaboration and show convincingly that language and translation problems feature strongly in the understanding and execution of the research project.

Another question pertinent to the early stages is about the sources of readings that a research engages in. Which books, papers or other sources are read and included in the thinking and the very early beginnings of conceptualization? Would it matter if ideas by French thinkers (Foucault, Bourdieu; see Bennett (2017) on the reception and translation of Foucault's work into Anglophone contexts) or German thinkers (Habermas, Heidegger) or Chinese thinkers (Confucius, Lao Tzu) or Greek thinkers (Aristotle, Socrates) are accessed and read in the original language or in translation? Or is it possible that the English language is by now so deeply engrained in the thinking of management academics that it suffices to 'carry' meanings of ideas and vocabularies from other languages? Is it gradually becoming a global language of management knowledge? But where would this leave audiences from practice or localities less well-resourced with access to English?

There are – to the best of my knowledge – no accounts within (inter-national) business and management that concern themselves with such meta-theoretical questions. There are, however, other sources that dig into the questions of languages, translation and what remains difficult to translate in the field of philosophy. There is a dictionary of untranslatables, a philosophical lexicon edited by French philosopher Barbara Cassin (2004), and translation editors Emily Apter, Jacques Lezra and Michael Wood; translators are Steven Rendall, Christian Hubert, Jeffrey Mehlman, Nathanael Stein and Michael Syrotinski. The dictionary contains essays and language perspectives about key philosophical traditions and vocabularies, about philosophies in trans-lation; it talks about the 'editorial liberties' taken (preface, p. xi) and 'the spectres of national subjects' (p. xii) – i.e. the dominant cultural frames that inform the understanding of key terms and vocabularies.

To provide an example; in the aforementioned philosophical dic-tionary there is an essay about the philosophical term *Ereignis* (English:

event) which is used by the German philosopher Heidegger as a *Leitwort* (nearest translation: *leading term*). In management research the nearest term is more likely to be *key concept*, though this does not capture the nuance that a *Leitwort* sets a stronger sense of trajectory than a key concept, from which analysis is more likely to fall out. Further questions arise: how is one to capture <u>das</u> *Ergebnis* (of an event) (English, result or outcome) when Heidegger also means <u>die</u> *Er-gebnis* as in English the giving yield.

Within German grammar, the gender has been changed from neutral (*das*) to feminine (*die*), a significant shift in meaning – an impossibility in the English language. And so it goes on. One also wonders what for example a Chinese doctoral student then makes of the teaching of research philosophies within UK universities, where there is very little awareness that traditions and terms such as critical pragmatism, grounded theory and discursive realities are difficult terms to understand for everyone, let alone for someone whose first language constructs the social world sometimes radically differently from English. Xian and Meng-Lewis (2018) have responded to the need to develop materials for non-native English researchers, in their case Chinese students, and have written a textbook about business research methods in which the key term of social science epistemology and methods are explained for this audience.

The writing strategy is based on including Chinese sentences and explanation of key research methodological terms informed by the authors' understanding that completing an evidence-based research project can be a big challenge for students who are 'confronted with culture and language difficulties, while trying to acquire sufficient knowledge to use various research methods and meet the academic requirements of overseas universities' (Xian & Meng-Lewis, 2018). This approach is still unusual both in terms of its important intent to provide a source that understands the needs of the readership as non- native English speakers and that learning for these students is beset by difficulties as 'English and Chinese are very dissimilar languages, and technical terms (e.g. positivism, grounded theory) have no direct translation in the Chinese language'. The social context of Chinese is not captured by Western authors and by providing Western examples, and the very notion of evidence-based research as the be all and end all of all social science research is also problematic within 'other' traditions. Thus, to return to the example of 'grounded theory' – translating it into Chinese cannot be resolved by merely finding or even inventing an equivalent word for it or using it as a loan word. This analytic technique is based on assumptions of having particular sets of empirical data and that these can be theorized from. In other traditions, my national one included to an extent, empirical data and interrogating the evidence are not as privileged as in the UK system of social science philosophy. Hence, understanding let alone applying grounded theory is based on a set of tacit assumptions of what makes 'good research'.

In summary, these are the beginnings of an argument that the early stages of the research journey, which may well be an interlingual one, requiring translation, disappear from the accessible accounts that are given about knowledge produced. Yet, benefits are to be had in the scrutiny of such processes as they provide the *Leitwörter* of what then becomes a research project, which remains to date a hidden aspect of knowledge generation.

Data collection and analysis (empirical)

In many research projects that straddle national boundaries, or which investigate global phenomena (e.g. global talent management; diversity practices) and in so far as these projects entail an empirical component, they are likely to yield data which is multilingual, i.e. raw data not presented in the English language. This poses a multitude of challenges for researchers and throws them back upon their own individual or collective language competence. Also, the selection of the research phenomena, the formulation of research questions and access to potential interviews are likely be influenced by the researchers' language skills (if working in a research team) (Chapman, Gajewska-De Mattes & Antouini, 2004).

In interview contexts in particular if rich data is sought, not having a language to communicate in easily can result in impoverished data – again, a phenomenon that is not discussed widely. Likewise, the use of translators or interpreters may produce disruption in terms of upsetting a natural and easy tempo of the exchange or create an additional layer of artificiality. So, whether the selected interview language is equally shared between interviewer and interviewee or whether the researcher or the interviewee has a linguistic advantage critically shapes the researcher–interviewee relationship (Marschand-Piekkarie & Reis, 2004; Welch & Piekkari, 2006).

Welch and Piekkari (2006) have conducted some research into language-questions as they play out within qualitative interviews. They range from decisions about the project language, where English appear to be the natural choice. Yet, when probed there are examples from international research collaborations, where this proved cumbersome and counterproductive as meaning remained incomprehensible for research team members who had no access to the language data, and it proved slow and costly to buy in appropriate translation services. It also enabled some researchers with additional control over data and its use. Likewise, decisions about the access language are important and this is often the local language (and not English). In such cases access negotiations depend on the local collaborator, if there is any or another intermediary or a translator. Welch and Piekkari (2006) also pose questions about the post-interview language, relating to data ana-lysis, there are potentially many different agents involved such as other native speakers (of the local language, reading the interview scripts), the local intermediary (which may also be the local researcher), pro-fessional interpreters or translators, language-skilled research students! None of these involvements of knowledge agents is without its ethical dilemmas, and none of it without its analytical consequences. All of these pose question over who controls the data and the meaning that is attributed to it.

Overall, the field of international management and business research is poorly equipped to deal with questions of how to think about and exe-cute international research. It involves 'a series of linguistic interactions and negotiations through which participants actively assemble a localized understanding' (Ryen, 2002, quoted in Welch & Piekkari, 2006, p. 431). Piekkari and Tietze (2016) write from a similar perspec-tive when they investigate the research process located in multinational corporations (MNCs). They take a strong political perspective on the overall process and see, in line with Westwood (2004, p. 56):

> methodology [is] as ineluctably embedded in ontological and epis-temological assumptions, as well as in the motivation and values of the research. These are in turn enfolded in as well as a historic-ally, institutionally and ideologically informed discursive context. … Research methods are not innocent: they are political.

In terms of gaining access, for example, they show how its safeguarding is a sometimes prolonged, protracted and precarious pro-cess, relying even on the mutuality of favours that are given or promised. Likewise, data collection in interviews, data analysis, exiting the field are steps that are imbued in the management of uneven relationships and in multilingual contexts, shaped strongly by the availability and compe-tence agents have with regard to activating language and translation, as are the stages of data analysis and evaluation. In their account Piekkari and Tietze (2016) stress the political nature of the research process, in particular multilingual settings such as a MNC.

Xian (2008) provides an extended example of her experience, based on her doctoral project, which included the translation of Chinese data (about the experiences of women entrepreneurs in China; thus, data included women's narratives about their life stories, feelings and attitudes) into the English language as her doctorate was gained at a British university. She advocates an approach whereby the interlingual translation process is seen as cultural translation and therefore as part of data analysis (rather than as a technical necessity). Translation of data was never straightforward for Xian due to linguistic differences between the English and Chinese language (e.g. Chinese language does not use tenses, or personal pronouns are not distinguished in the verbal form).

Second, the socio-cultural context of Chinese women's positions cannot be translated straightforwardly, in particular if it is expressed through using idioms, culturally embedded mythologies, proverbs and sayings. From thereon, Xian discussed how to address such language/ cultural differences and ask what is the translator's role in the research process, with the latter's being imperative for the creation of know-ledge across languages and in the struggle to remain authentic to the researched location, while acknowledging the need for a readership beyond the local language. For Xian, the magic component to achieve this delicate balance lies in understanding and utilizing translation as a conceptual, meta-theoretical way of thinking about international management research, as well as in laying open the details of the interlingual translation process itself, which in the case of her study involved both herself as researcher-translators and other native Chinese speakers.

Another example of an empirical study set within an MNC with US headquarters and located in a Polish subsidiary (Ciuk, James & Śliwa, 2019) sees interlingual translation decisions aligned to micro-political processes and, importantly, it is also constitutive of the relationship between headquarters and subsidiary. Translating agents include bilingual Polish managers who occupy the dual role of translator and implementer of new practices. Interlingual translation decisions provide important performance as they both direct and conclude the reception of incoming new ideas and practices. In this regard, Piekkari, Tietze and Koskinen (2020) argue that interlingual translation is a necessary and crucial communicative act through which multilingual organizations are talked, written and translated into being.

It was stated that this book focuses more strongly on research concerned with the hermeneutic process of understanding how meaning is generated in international research and what role language diversity and translation play in these. However, it needs to be stressed that the same issues hold fore over quantitatively based research such as operationalized through surveys, for example. Usunier (2011) speaks explicitly to the case of quantitatively based cross-cultural management research and questions the assumed neutral-instrumental view of language the vast majority of such studies are based on. He posits that language differences can be used to reveal specific facets of meaning within cultures, with etymology as the study of sources and development of words, providing insight into lexically relevant concepts and to what extent they are the same across languages/cultures and to what extent and why they differ. He proposes, amongst others, a 'comparative etymological approach' (p. 317) of key business concepts, which needs to inform quantitative surveys as early as the stage of research design. Likewise, Fan and Harzing (2020) draw attention to the usefulness of experiments in language-based research as a means to create causality and a strong test about how reliable a theory is.

Epistemology

The underpinning epistemology of the majority of international management studies can be described as hinging on an equivalent paradigm (Chidlow, Plakoyannaki & Welch, 2014), which means that in cross-cultural or cross-language projects, translation is used to establish identical meanings across languages. It has been established in previous chapters why this is not possible. The main method of quantitative international business studies is shown to be based on back translation (Brislin, 1970) with a view to eliminate translation errors. The direction of translation is, of course, mainly from the local language to English. Their findings show that back-translation approaches and equivalence thinking dominate international business research to avoid distortion of data or to ensure, assure or secure equivalence as far as possible.

Qualitative international business research remains mainly silent on language and does not account for the translation process in the reporting documents. Partly, this is because there are no standardized procedures to do so; partly this is because the opportunities to use translation as an important part of data analysis have not yet penetrated the collective thought processes of researchers and thus are not incorporated in writing and publication practices. The authors also propose to move away from the equivalent paradigm, and to cultivate a closer relationship between international business and management research and translation studies, where the role of the translator and the translation process is discussed in terms of documenting and accounting for translation decisions, making visible the translator's role in the research account and reflecting and accounting for the processes and methods used. Finally, in drawing attention to the process of translation as changing the data, bringing in local perspectives and so forth is also seen to address the cultural politics inscribed in text production in so far as difference does not become erased, appropriated or exoticized.

Publication practices

In previous chapters publication practices have already been discussed in the light of them being based on assumptions that English can carry, express and reproduce all possible meanings that exist in the social world. Such assumptions have been characterized as essentialist and universalist and have been associated with the hegemonic reproduction of mainly Westernized canons of knowledge, privileging the perspectives and identities of knowledge centres and knowledge workers located in the influential Western-centric cores (i.e. the US and the UK). Management scholars have begun to take issues with these positions from a specific language and translation perspective (e.g. Boussebaa & Brown, 2017; Steyaert & Janssens, 2013; Boussebaa & Tienari, 2019; Tietze, 2004, 2018; Wilmot & Tietze, 2021, *forthcoming*) and begun to highlight the incongruities, paradoxes, consequences and injustices of such monolingual thinking and language use. In particular, there are consequences for the knowledge itself and also for the well-being of knowledge workers, whose identities are (re) constructed in line with Anglo-Saxon preferences and perspectives on what constitutes valid knowledge (see in particular Boussebaa & Brown, 2017; Tietze & Dick, 2013).

The main concerns about these practices have already been rehearsed; therefore, this brief section contains only some pointers into alternative ways of ordering the knowledge production processes within international management research. Steyaert and Janssens (2013), for example, question the unreflexive use of English in management and organization studies and the current status quo in multilingual scholarship as woefully underequipped to respond constructively to construct the world through a multiplicity of languages. Tietze (2018) provides some concrete pointers beyond cultivating the integration of translation studies thinking into international management research. These include, amongst others: (a) to institutionalize translation through the establishment of reporting mechanisms about the translation process within research accounts; (b) the incorporation of interlingual translation as part of data analysis in particular in qualitative approaches and (c) the institutionalization of translation in terms of academic stakeholders who can generate awareness and promote practices among journal editors and editorial boards about the opportunities and imperatives to include translation aspects into publication practices (see also Harzing & Metz, 2012).

Conclusion

In previous chapters it was shown that a body of work exists that has developed sensitivity of how languages and their use inform research into international management. This body of work is now crossing disciplinary boundaries into other fields of inquiry (e.g. Evans, 2018; Lillis & Curry, 2014; Kettunen, 2017), and it is also turning to translation as a means and theme to understand multilingual phenomena in and across work communities. This body of work has a strong empirical base, perhaps at the expense of debates about methodologies in particular. In this regard it can be said that there is no consolidated understanding about questions of research design and research philosophies for multilingual research. In a way the main aim for this book is to provide such a source to inform and to stimulate more detailed works. In this regard the reviewed pieces in the previous section are exemplary and innovative, but so far, they have not formed into a corpus of work. How this formation can be propelled forward is the theme of the concluding chapter.

In concluding, it can be stated that to date there are available sources that have engaged with the epistemological, political and methodological questions that arise when conducting research into multilingual contexts or when discussing the knowledge production process itself. However, these have not as yet amalgamated into protocols on how to report on language/translation decisions within reporting structures, into a deep debate about the philosophical underpinnings of research traditions and so forth. What we have are scattered pieces by individual scholars who have taken an interest in these matters. This book is an attempt to provide one source to initiate a change in orientation and practice in business and management research. In Chapter 5 some possibilities for the future and a vision of hospitality will be expressed.

References

Bennett, K. (2017). Foucault in English. The politics of exoticization, *Target*, *29*, 2, 224–245.
Bhabha, H. (2004). *The location of culture,* London: Routledge Classics.
Boussebaa, M. and Brown, A. (2017). Englishization, identity regulation and imperialism, *Organization Studies*, *38*, 1, 7–29.

Boussebaa, M. and Tienari, J. (2019). Englishization and the politics of knowledge production in management studies. *Journal of Management Inquiry*, *30*, 1, 59–67.

Brislin, R. W. (1970). Back-translation for cross-cultural research, *Journal of Cross-Cultural Psychology*, *1*, 3, 185–216.

Cassin, B. (Ed.). (2004). *Dictionary of untranslatables. A philosophical lexicon.* Princeton: Princeton University Press.

Chapman, M., Gajewska-De Mattes, H. and Antouini, C. (2004). The ethnographic international business researcher. Misfit or trailblazer? In R. Piekkari and C. Welch (Eds.). *Handbook of qualitative research methods for international business*, (pp. 287–305). Cheltenham: Edward Elgar.

Chidlow, A., Plakoyiannaki, E. and Welch, C. (2014). Translation in cross-language international business research: Beyond equivalence, *Journal of International Business Studies*, *45*, 562–582.

Ciuk, S., James, P. and Śliwa, M. (2019). Micropolitical dynamics of interlingual translation processes in an MNC subsidiary, *British Journal of Management*, *30*, 4, 926–942.

Evans, L. (2018). Language, translation and accounting: Towards a critical research agenda, *Accounting, Auditing and Accountability Journal*, *31*, 7, 1844–1876.

Fan, S. and Harzing, A. W. (2020). Moving beyond the baseline: Exploring the potential of experiments in language research. In S. Horn, P. Lecomte, P. and S. Tietze (Eds.). *Managing multilingual workplaces. Methodological, empirical and pedagogic perspectives*, (pp. 9–28). Routledge: Abingdon.

Fougère, M. and Moulettes, A. (2012). Disclaimers, dichotomies and disappearances in international business textbooks: A postcolonial deconstruction, *Management Learning*, *43*, 1, 5–24.

Grey, C. (2010). Organizing studies: publications, politics and polemic, *Organization Studies*, *31*, 6, 677–694.

Harzing, A. W. and Metz, I. (2012). Explaining geographic diversity of editorial boards: The role of conference participation and English language skills, *European Journal of International Management*, *6*, 6, 697–715.

Holland, R. (2002) Globospeak? Questioning text on the role of English as a global language, *Language and Intercultural Communication*, *2*, 1, 5–24.

Jack, G. (2004). Language(s), intercultural communication and the machinations of global capital: Towards a dialectical critique, *Language and Intercultural Communication*, *4*, 3, 121–133.

Jack, G. and Westwood, R. (2006). Postcolonialism and the politics of qualitative research in international business, *Management International Review*, *46*, 4, 481–501.

Jack, G., Westwood, R., Srinivas, N. and Sardar, Z. (2011). Deepening, broadening, and re-asserting a post-colonial interrogative space in organization studies, *Organization*, *18*, 3, 275–302.

Kettunen, J. (2017). Interlingual translation of the international financial reporting standards as institutional work, *Accounting, Organization and Society*, *56*, 38–54.

Lillis, T. and Curry, J. (2014). *Academic writing in a global context. The politics and practices of publishing in English.* London: Taylor and Francis.
Marschan-Piekkari, R. and Reis, C. (2004). Language and languages in cross-cultural interviewing. In R. Marschan-Piekkari and C. Welch (Eds.). *Handbook for qualitative research for international business*, (pp. 224–243). Cheltenham: Edward Elgar.
Meriläinen, A., Tienari, J., Thomas, R. and Davies, A. (2008). Hegemonic academic practices: Experiences of publishing from the periphery, *Organization*, *15*, 4, 584–597.
Mika, J. P. and O'Sullivan, J. G. (2014). A Māori approach to management: Contrasting traditional and modern Māori management practices in Aotearoa New Zealand, *Journal of Management and Organization*, *20*, 5, 648–670.
Miller, D. B. (2016). *The girl in green.* London: Faber & Faber.
Piekkari, R. and Tietze, S. (2016). Micropolitical behavior in the multinational enterprise: A language perspective. In Alain Verbeke, Robert Van Tulder, and Sarianna Lundan, (Eds.). *Multinational enterprises, markets and institutional diversity: Progress in international business*, (pp. 259–277). Bingley: Emerald.
Piekkari, R., Tietze, S. and Koskinen, K. (2020). Metaphorical and interlingual translation in moving organizational practices across languages. *Organization Studies*, *41*, 9, 1311–1332.
Ryen, A. (2002) Cross-cultual interviewing. In J. F. Gubrium and J. A. Holstein (Eds.). *Handbook of interview research: Contexts and methods*, (pp. 335–353). Thousand Oaks: Sage.
Said, E. W. (1978). *Orientalism*, new edition, London: Penguin.
Steyaert, C. and Janssens, M. (2013). Multilingual scholarship and the paradox of translation and language in management and organization studies, *Organization, 20*, 1, 131–142.
Thomas, R., Tienari, J., Davies, A. and Meriläinen, S. (2009). Let's talk about "us". A reflexive account of a cross-cultural research collaboration, *Journal of Management Inquiry*, *18*, 4, 313–324.
Tietze, S. (2004). Spreading the management gospel – in English, *Language and Intercultural Communication*, *4*, 3, 175–189.
Tietze, S. (2018). Multilingual research, monolingual publications: management scholarship in English only?, *European Journal of International Management*, *12*, 1–2, 28–45.
Tietze, S. and Dick, P. (2013). The victorious English language: Hegemonic practices in the management academy. *Journal of Management Inquiry*, *22*, 1, 122–134.
Üsdiken, B. (2010). Between contending perspectives and logics: organizational studies in Europe, *Organization Studies*, *31*, 6, 715–735.
Usunier, J. C. (2011). Language as a resource to assess cross-cultural equivalence in quantitative management research, *Journal of World Business*, *46*, 3, 314–319.

Welch, C. and Piekkari, R. (2006). Crossing language boundaries: Qualitative interviewing in international business, *Management International Review*, *46*, 417–437.

Westwood, R. (2004). Towards a postcolonial research paradigm in international business and comparative management, In R. Marschan-Piekkari and C. Welch (Eds.). *Handbook of qualitative methods for international business*, (pp. 56–83). Cheltenham: Edward Elgar.

Westwood, R. (2006). International business and management studies as an orientalist discourse: A postcolonial critique, *Critical Perspectives on International Business*, *2*, 2, 91–113.

Westwood, R. and Jack, G. (2007). Manifesto for a post-colonial international business and management studies: A provocation, *Critical Perspectives on International Business*, *3*, 3, 246–265.

Wilmot, N. and Tietze, S. (2021, forthcoming). Englishization and the politics of translation. *Critical Perspectives on International Business*. https://doi.org/10.1108/cpoib-03-2020-0019

Xian, H. (2008). Lost in translation? Language, culture and the roles of translator in cross-cultural management research, *Qualitative Research in Organizations and Management: An International Journal*, *3*, 3, 231–245.

Xian, H. and Meng-Lewis, Y. (2018). *Business research methods for Chinese students. A practical guide to your research project*. London and Thousand Oaks: Sage.

5 Developing global literacy for management research

Translation is not a straightforward enterprise as absolute equivalence between languages does not exist. However, efforts to translate are efforts to communicate and to share meaning. In this regard the very *Sperrigkeit* of words (German: bulkiness; however, a *Sperre* is a barrier to something and being *sperrig* can also express the quality of a deliberate refusal to fit easily) and of translation offers a space to create understanding across human groups and groupings. This space is all the more valuable as it has to be worked for:

> Translation became a necessary human activity. When there was not an equivalent word for something in another language, people had to settle for second best, which was how they came to understand the importance of charity as well as precision. When they could not say exactly what they meant, they let the frustration of that soften them toward other people who could not say exactly what they meant either.
>
> (Brown Taylor, 2018, p. 181)

This book opened with a question about the essence of global or international business and management research. It was proposed that the common denominator of this research is the English language as the adopted, practiced and taken-for-granted language of all knowledge. This position was shown as untenable for a variety of reasons that were developed across the previous chapters. Critical management scholars, including those taking strong postcolonial positions and those with a particular interest in the constitution of organizations through language and communication, have begun to challenge some assumptions upon which contemporary management knowledge is founded – frequently these relate to the geopolitical positions of researcher and researched and the historical inequalities that continue in slightly changed disguises up to our times.

Thus, these scholars call for a reconsideration of what it means to do research in global contexts and consequently to develop practices that will lead to a reconfiguration of the knowledge production process (e.g. Westwood & Jack, 2007). In a similar vein, Bell, Kothiyal and Willmott (2017) call for a 'reconfiguration of management research on a global scale [which] requires development and application of diverse methods, such as those based on narrative knowledge and storytelling (Kaomea, 2016, quoted in Bell *et al.* p. 534) (...) with a view to include management researchers located on the periphery as bricoleurs (Denzin and Lincoln, 2005), drawing research methods creatively to bear witness to report their experiences and in doing so challenge the status quo. According to Bell *et al.* (2017), the use of English as a dominant code of representation in international publishing reinscribes power relations associated with centre-peripheral positioning. In some ways the existing studies quoted in the previous chapter (e.g. Boussebaa & Brown, 2017; Mika & O'Sullivan, 2014; Xian, 2008) are expressive of this advocated approach with drawing on translation studies being one of the means to bricolage and represent more fully peripheral experiences and 'other languages'.

This chapter then aims to take forward these calls for reconfigurations of global management research, by providing some pointers into how it may be achieved and what it means for individual and collective practices and resources that are needed.

Developing global literacy

Chapter 2 opens with a quote taken from an autobiography of Barbara Ehrenreich (2014). She compares what it means to work in or live in another language as 'losing your grip on reality. That is why it is so hard, so soul-destroying if not resolved, so liberating, if understood'. In the empirical work informing the publications Tietze (2009) and Tietze and Dick (2013), I talked in depth to a number of non-native English management academics, all of whom struggled to express their research findings, their theorizing and the nuances of their qualitative research in English. Some of the quotes did not make it into the published papers as I was not quite ready at the time to appreciate the deeper meanings of what people tried to express when they said about their research 'it is simply not true if it is not in English' or 'it [translated text into English] makes it feel unreal' or 'my respondents are like lies when I translate it' (here talking about translation of Italian language data gained during an ethnography and translated into English).

These comments resonate with Ehrenreich's description of the nexus of ties between language and one's grip on reality. In the experiences of my respondents, it was soul-destroying; yet in my own professional experience, in particular as a younger researcher, I found the experience with struggling over English words and their meanings oddly satisfying and uplifting.

Overall, however, management scholars 'don't get this' – with 'this' being what it means to be an alien in a knowledge/language world which one is supposed to master and command. In this regard the literacy of management academics is underdeveloped. Of course, for most scholars, whether native speakers of English or not, writing is hard work and learning one's craft (Watson, 1994) is a slow process. To repeat, it is a hard craft for everyone to learn, whether one is working in and through one's native language or not. However, it is at the same time more than the acquisition of a technical skill; rather it is entering a mode of thinking and creating perspectives on knowledge.

Global literacy

Alison Phipps (2019) provides a text about what it means to and how to write without borders in your mind, and in doing so to decolonize multilingualism. In the introduction she comments on a wonderful, rich and formidable source, *The Handbook of Critical and Indigenous Methodologies*, edited by Denzin, Lincoln and Smith (2008). A book that is 'cock full of essays presenting the perspectives of indigenous people' (p. 2), yet with little or no reference to English or multilingualism. Language, one assumes, is seen to be a mechanistic vehicle or carrier of meaning, rather than the energy through which cultures are breathed and talked into being. Thus, the stance taken here is that to develop global literacy in academic writing; it is critical to engage with multilingualism (including English). A critique of critical management studies, including postcolonial approaches, is that they are monolingual in orientation – partly through necessity as their reach is beyond national, cultural and language boundaries, but also because of a lack of awareness and understanding of why language is of central relevance to their project.

Hasan (2003, p. 433) states that we are witnessing

> the deployment of language in a struggle to control the very picture of reality ... [and that] to understand how globalization might affect our lives, we will need a form of literacy that goes beyond simple interpretation and to reflection on the social significance of acts or meaning: Literacy must enable one to decide whose meanings are voiced in which acts of semiosis and for whose benefit.

The use of a globalizing variety of English has since the post-1989s, according to Hasan, superseded the ordinary speakers use of English, and propelled forward the resemantification (i.e. meaning change, meaning appropriation) by offering concepts of managerialism, the ideology of capitalism and acts as a resource for speakers' acts of meaning and practices in the world. In many ways Hasan's argument aligns with Philippson's notion of linguistic imperialism, with Hasan stressing the 'inherent flexibility of meaning' as offering the opportunity for powerful (global) elites to foreground and progress the meaning systems most closely aligned with the advancement of their vested interests. In Hasan's terms then having competence in a global literacy enables the sceptical scrutiny of how and why language is used to generated meaning through which, in turn, actions become grounded, legitimate and possible.

Lillis and Curry (2014) comment on academic text production as a social practice, where texts are not seen to exist in isolation, but are bound up with what people do within respective social, economic, historical and political contexts. They therefore see academic writing as rooted in specific cultural traditions of ways of constructing knowledge, with English being a main resource of knowledge construction in management and business research (Canagarajah, 2001). In other words, texts and contexts cannot be separated. The papers and chapters, the books and reports written and published by management academics are inscribed, often invisibly, with contexts of where, for whom and how they were produced. Lillis and Curry's work is located in new literary studies, where such knowledge production and practice are seen to be interrelated. They also note that the privileged position of English globally and the impact of this privileged position on knowledge making are less widely discussed within this particular community. The next section therefore provides some examples from (international) management literatures that disrupt or challenge the language status quo. They are described here as providing some ideas and stimulation about how changes in the international business/management communities could be propelled forward.

Decentring text production

Mila and O'Sullivan (2014) write about a Māori approach to management drawing on discourses of indigeneity, post-colonialism and critical management studies. They show Maori management as a distinctive form of management within Aotearoa New Zealand. While drawing on one of the classic authors of management (Fayol), and while their paper is written in English, it is also brim-full with Maori terms and language, with explaining their meanings, traditions and how they could guide an understanding of the 'other', which is in this particular paper clearly the Western ways and concepts of management that are inscribed in the English language. The paper provides an example of reversing the normal (hegemonic) order by fore-fronting the trajectory of Maori traditions that are left visible through words and sentences in the body of the text and also in figures and tables. It requires patience from the reader and a willingness to read thoroughly and slowly. It disrupts the smoothly spinning wheels of our mental minds and mindscapes.

Gabrois and Nentwich's (2020) paper on the dynamics of privilege and using English in a MNC setting is preambled by two abstracts, one in English, one in French. While the reading of the paper itself does not make the same demands on the reader as Mila and O'Sullivan's paper does, it nevertheless causes a brief interruption of the reading process, perhaps a half-formulated idea or a quick glance at both abstracts and wondering why this is a practice within this journal (*Canadian Journal of Administrative Sciences*) – which is likely to have to do with the bi-lingual status of much of Canada, but which is also a deliberate choice of acknowledging both languages.

Langinier and Ehrhart's (2019) paper is titled *Quand le local rencontre le global: Comment l'introduction de l'anglais déstabilise les pratiques de translanguaging dans une entrepresie frontalière* or *Cuando el local encuentra al global: como la introudcción del inglés desestabiliza las práctictas translanguaing en una compañía fronteriza* or *When local meets global: how introducing English destabilizes translanguaging practise in a cross-border organization* (journal: *Management International*). In reading it is possible to skip over the three titles – in writing them it is not! – likewise, there is an abstract in English, French and Spanish as reminders that the content of the paper is about issues of multilingualism and that it claims a rightful position in the minds of its readership as just so.

Gaggiotti and Marre (2017) analyse the words for understandings and enactment of leadership in an Italo-Latin multinational corporation. In their study and text, they present different words for leader and leadership and also explain the different meanings attached to these contexts, ranging from historical usages to deeply micro ones linked to the particular local-corporate cultures at the researched settings. It is a study that uses in the widest sense a representational strategy based on the use of loan word, thereby always implying that something is loaned and therefore different from the prevailing context and situation. The authors also use a strategy that leaves visible the local national language words and uses these to launch and guide interpretation, explanation and analysis. It is not unlike the approach articulated by Xian (2008), which was discussed in the previous chapter, in that using 'foreignness' is used to achieve the dual goal of leaving intact and respecting local traditions, while rendering research findings and ideas accessible to a wider, non-local audience.

To varying degrees and extents these authors use what can be summarized as a writing strategy based on *foreignization* – as opposed to domestication, which is the overwhelming approach used in both critical and mainstream management research. These terms derive from trans-lation studies and Lawrence Venuti has articulated them in particular for literature and literary studies (1993 and 2008) as translation strat-egies of domestication and foreignization. They address the question of how much a translation assimilates a foreign text to the translating language and culture, and how much it rather signals the differences of that text. Venuti is one of the most cited translation studies scholars within management studies, and his definition of domestication strat-egies is helpful to understand the use of English to domesticate (or even to sanitize) the 'other' out of the published text. Foreignization strat-egies of writing and representation integrate, leave visible or use the 'other' in the published text to draw attention to its existence, claim its right and rightfulness and use also in quite a pragmatic sense as a part of deepening understanding of the researched settings.

Foreignization as a practice is related to the development of some reflexivity about the role of English in text production (Steyaert & Janssens, 2013).

Whether the impetus derived initially from frustration about having to find equivalent words and meanings when translating data or ideas into English for publication purposes, or as a deliberate stance to include 'the other' into research accounts, the result is an increasing awareness of what it means to conduct multilingual research. This awareness about the decisions made in the overall research process as much as towards the writing up stages is *linguistic reflexivity* (see also Horn, Lecomte & Tietze, 2020). It brings into sharp relief underlying patterns of thinking and practice that otherwise remain unquestioned. In this regard exer-cising linguistic reflexivity links up with the exercise of critical reflexivity as in multilingual research issues of representation play out through the writing strategies the authors select. Lillis and Curry (2014, p. 6) advo-cate to consider the geographical (local, regional and national contexts and institutions), geolinguistic (the languages used or not used in the production process) and geopolitical dimensions (policies and practices influencing research and its evaluation at national and supranational

levels) as a response to understanding the knowledge production process. An interesting and relevant example they provide pertains to the
keywords of this book – as also reflected in its title, international management research – and the opening question, what is international?
Towards the end of this particular text, it is now possible to answer this
question more extensively. Leaning on Lillis and Curry, *international*
is a widely spread currency in public discourse and in policy making.
In the UK, *international* is a hall mark of high-quality research and
used as a value-bestowing descriptor (even for pieces that are not in
the strict sense crossing national boundaries in content or approach) in
research assessment cycles on the basis of which resources are allocated
and reputations are made. Lillis and Curry also point out that international is a sliding signifier (2014, p. 6) coming 'to index far more than
concerning two or more nations, but that "in the context of academic
publishing ... [it is] used as a proxy for 'English medium'", and together
"English" and "international" constitute an important indexical cluster
used to signal "high quality"'.

It is possible to change the institutional practices that inform such
existence of powerful indexical clusters. The studies and examples used
in this book point to a shift in how to think about, execute and report
multilingual research. In this regard there are many examples available
from which to learn from and absorb into existing institutional practices
with a view to instigate change. Lillis and Curry point to the mediation
process between the writing of a text and its publication. Mediators are
agents such as editors, critical readers, members of reading groups and
also the facilitators and hosts of the increasing number of workshops,
writing retreats, reading groups or doctoral symposia that can shape
and influence practice and who broker texts. They are the literary
brokers identified by Lillis and Curry and whose views, decisions and
communications yield considerable influence on the writing strategies
of researchers and what is deemed as valid or not so valid knowledge
(Tietze & Dick, 2013). In this regard journal editors and the compos-
ition of editorial boards are important agents who set trajectories for
text production. These stakeholders may be the people to talk to with
a view to develop protocols on how to report about multilingual data
sets, how to include and conceptualize ideas and concepts not available
in English.

Change is also needed in the way future researchers are trained and
equipped. Management and business research mainly draw on the social
sciences in terms of the methods and methodologies it employs. There
is to date no textbook for research students that endeavours to capture
the available methods from a multilingual and translation perspective.

Such a resource is needed for the community of researchers if multilingual research is to be embedded within its research practices, and from thereon new traditions can be developed.

Translation

It is proposed that translation as an approach and a means to understand, analyse and conceptualize multilingual research projects offers an avenue to develop perspectives on international themes and contexts of research that are currently neglected. In this regard social science methods and their application within multilingual research will be innovated, rather than replaced by a set of new methods or methodologies. This is not to say that social science researchers, which includes the majority of management researchers, could not loan and use concepts from translation studies (e.g. Piekkari, Tietze & Koskinen, 2020; Ciuk, James & Śliwa, 2019) or from the arts and humanities (e.g. Outila, Piekkari & Michaelova, 2020) with a view to broaden and deepen the repertoire of available research techniques and tools. Likewise, using visual data or materials (Shortt & Warren, 2012) or other forms of representation may be means to integrate more fully and more openly traditions and perspectives that are not always enshrined in the written word (Boxenbaum, Jones & Meyer, 2018).

Translation is an adequate, for now, response to the dilemmas and complexities posed by engagement with the peripheral 'other', with languages that express and create meanings and worldviews. Montgomery (2000, p. 1) purports that

> As a textual reality, the history of science in any single tongue involves many matters of coinage, the creation of vocabularies ... A nomenclature is built from thousands of such selections; it leaks history at every pore.

Such coded knowledge becomes mobile in two ways, either there is an agreement to use a shared language (in our times this is English) with the consequences outlined in this book; or which is Montgomery's thesis, epochs of great intellectual advancement are based on the mobilization of knowledge, often quite unexpectedly in particular historical periods. 'What makes it possible to cross boundaries of time, place and language? ... "Translation"' (pp. 2–3), which includes single acts of translating words and texts from language A to language B, but it also includes the wider and deeper transformation of knowledge when it is 'given a whole new context and voice', when it becomes movement of ideas through which change and transformation is achieved (Montgomery, 2000, pp. 2–5).

Westney and Piekkari (2020) provide one such example where they espouse a translation framework to track, and re-frame the knowledge transfer of manufacturing knowledge and practices (knowledge translation) from Japan to the US (initially). They posit that there must have been many thousands of translation acts performed by many different translators to gain momentum into a sharing of and shift in practices pertaining to the manufacturing of cars. Not an easy feat given the cultural distance between Japan and the US, and truly revolutionizing given the central importance of transport in many societies – achieved through translation of knowledge and practice over time.

Paul Ricoeur wrote a philosophical book about translation, 'Sur la traduction', which was published in 2004 and came out in English (on translation) in 2006, translated by Eileen Brennan. Ricoeur argues that all languages mediate between a human speaker and a world of meaning, actual and possible, which we can speak and write about. As there are many different languages, humans are faced with a double duty of translation, intra to themselves and external to and with others. Translation is both intralingual and interlingual. It thus provides a sense-making mechanism within one language and across two or more. It is both inward facing, as we must self-translate to ourselves, as well as outward facing as we translate between each other, both within one language and across several. Within Ricoeur's take, translation is indicative of the ontological acts of speaking of translating oneself.

The existence of different languages requires an even more demanding encounter with the language other. It 'requires us to abandon the dream of a perfect language - and of a global translation without residues of shades of meanings'. Kearney (2007, p. 151) writes: '[We] are called to make our language part of the strangers' clothes at the same time as we invite the stranger to step into the fabric of our own speech'. This invitation of strangeness is therefore an act of linguistic hospitality – an invitation to forgo the lure of omnipotence, e.g. the illusion of a total translation that would provide a perfect replica of the original. Instead, it asks us to respect the fact that the semantic and syntactic fields of two language are not the same.

These ideas about translation resonate with the examples of this book, where authors had to work through otherness, the *Sperrigkeit* of words meets with the fluidity of meanings.

Working with translation includes asking questions about which position they are writing from and what they consider to be the normal point of reference. Working with translation is therefore sometimes an unsettling experience, as any sincere response to language plurality involves an up-rooting of one's own place in the order of things.

References

Bell, E., Kothiyal, N. and Willmot, H. (2017). Methodology-as-technique and the meaning of rigour in globalized management research, *British Journal of Management*, *28*, 534–550.

Boussebaa, M. and Brown, A. (2017). Englishization, identity regulation and imperialism, *Organization Studies*, *38*, 1, 7–29.

Boxenbaum, E., Jones, C. and Meyer, R. E. (2018). Towards and articulation of the material and visual turn in organization studies, *Organization Studies*, *39*, 5–6, 597–616.

Brown-Taylor, B. (2018). *Holy envy: Finding god in the faith of others*. Norwich: Canterbury Press.

Canagarajah, A. S. (2001). Non-discursive requirements in academic publishing, material resources of periphery scholars, and the politics of knowledge production. *Written Communication*, *13*, 4, 435–472.

Ciuk, S., James, P. and Śliwa, M. (2019). Micropolitical dynamics of interlingual translation processes in an MNC subsidiary, *British Journal of Management*. *30*, 4, 926–942.

Denzin, N. and Lincoln, Y. (2005). 'The discipline and practice of qualitative research'. In Denzin, N. and Lincoln, Y. (eds), Handbook of Qualitative Research, pp. 1-32. Thousand Oaks CA: Sage.

Denzin, N. K., Lincoln, Y. S. and Smith, L. T. (Eds.). (2008). *Handbook of critical and indigenous methodologies*. London: Sage.

Ehrenreich, B. (2014). *Living with a wild God: A nonbeliever's search for the truth about everything*. London: Granta Books Publishing.

Gabrois, C. and Nentwich, J. (2020). The dynamics of privilege: How employees of a multinational corporation construct and contest the privileging effects of English proficiency. *Canadian Journal of Administrative Science*, *1*, 1–15.

Gaggiotti, H. and Marre, D. (2017). The words leader/lider and their resonances in an Italo-Latin American multinational corporation. *Leadership*, *13*, 2, 194–214.

Hasan, R. (2003). Globalization, literacy and ideology, *World Englishes*, *22*, 4, 433–448.

Horn, S., Lecomte, P. and Tietze, S. (2020) (Eds.). *Managing the multilingual workplace: Methodological, empirical and pedagogic perspectives*. Abington: Routledge.

Kaomea, J. (2016). Qualitative analysis as Ho'oku'iku'I or bricolage: teaching emancipatory indigenous research in postcolonial Hawaii, *Qualitative Inquiry*, *22*, 99–106.

Kearney, R. (2007). Paul Ricoeur and the hermeneutics of translation. *Research in Phenomenology*, *37*, 2, 147–159.

Langinier, H. and Ehrhard, S. (2019). When local meets global: How introducing English destabilizes translanguaging practices in a cross-border organization, *Management International, 1*, 1–14.

Lillis, T. and Curry, J. (2014). *Academic writing in a global context. The politics and practices of publishing in English.* London: Taylor and Francis.

Mika, J. P. and O'Sullivan, J. G. (2014). A Māori approach to management: Contrasting traditional and modern Māori management practices in Aotearoa New Zealand, *Journal of Management and Organization, 20,* 5, 648–670.

Montgomery, S. L. (2000). *Science in translation. Movements of knowledge through cultures and time.* Chicago and London: University of Chicago Press.

Outila, V., Piekkari, R. and Mihailova, I. (2020). How to research 'empowerment' in Russia: Absence, equivalence and method. In S. Horn, P. Lecomte and S. Tietze (Eds.). *Managing multilingual workplaces. Methodological, empirical and pedagogic perspectives,* (pp. 29–44). Abingdon: Routledge.

Phipps, A. (2019). *Decolonising multilingualism. Struggles to decreate*, Bristol: Multilingual Matters.

Piekkari, R., Tietze, S. and Koskinen, K. (2020). Metaphorical and interlingual translation in moving organizational practices across languages. *Organization Studies, 41,* 9, 1311–1332.

Ricoeur, P. (2004). *Sur la traduction.* Paris: Bayard.

Shortt, H. and Warren, S. (2012). Fringe benefits: Valuing the visual in hairdressers' identity work, *Visual Studies, 27*, 1, 18–34.

Steyaert, C. and Janssens, M. (2013). Multilingual scholarship and the paradox of translation and language in management and organization studies, *Organization, 20*, 1, 131–142.

Tietze, S. (2009). The work of management academics: An English language perspective, *English for Specific Purposes, 2*, 371–386.

Tietze, S. and Dick, P. (2013). The victorious English language: Hegemonic practices in the management academy. *Journal of Management Inquiry, 22,* 1, 122–134.

Venuti, L. (1993). Translation as cultural politics: Regimes of domestication in English, *Textual Practice, 7,* 2, 208–223.

Venuti, L. (2008). *The translator's invisibility: A history of translation,* 2nd edition, Abingdon: Routledge.

Watson. T. (1994). Rhetoric, discourse and argument in organizational sensemaking. A reflexive tale, *Organization Studies, 6*, 3, 805–821.

Westney, E. and Piekkari, R. (2020). Reversing the translation flow: Moving organizational practices from Japan to the U.S., *Journal of Management Studies, 57*, 57–86.

Westwood, R. and Jack, G. (2007). Manifesto for a post-colonial international business and management studies: A provocation, *Critical Perspectives on International Business, 3*, 3, 246–265.

Xian, H. (2008). Lost in translation? Language, culture and the roles of translator in cross-cultural management research, *Qualitative Research in Organizations and Management: An International Journal, 3*, 3, 231–245.

6 Conclusion
On being spoken and being written

Writing carries its own epistemology as when thoughts are turned into words and texts, they are bestowed with a degree of permanent and stable meaning, even within research traditions that underline the inherent flexibility and malleability of the word-meaning nexus. They materialize into bodies of knowledge, based on written texts. It is an utterly modern enterprise inscribed with assumptions of authorship, agency and about knowledge that resides unproblematically in written texts: Prometheus bound. Heather Höpfl (2000, p. 104) describes normal scientific writing as a patriarchal linear project springing from a fear of contamination with the Other's embodied spilling into the text, turning all otherness into abstraction and thus regulating it away. While including the language other (in ways discussed in previous chapters) in texts is not a panacea to patriarchal writing projects, it is a beginning to disrupt text production in such a way as to draw attention to other ways of talking, speaking and writing – to ways in which we communicate and generate and share knowledge.

It has been the contention of this book that within (international) management words and texts and meanings are mainly monolingual, and that consequent manifestations of texts into bodies of knowledge are biased towards the English language and the values, history and usages inscribed in it. In this regard the English language binds knowledge in particular ways.

However, even the very essence of this book which challenges the monolingual status of management research is based on notions of the author as agent who, faced with the multilingual life worlds she wants to explore, understand, explain, needs to make choices relating to the representation of such multilingual voices in her research account. Such ability to make choices, however, is presupposed on the awareness of the researcher that these choices matter and are important and, on the possibility, to integrate these choices into the written text. Overall, it is still difficult to do the latter as the whole of management studies is blissfully ignorant, if not downright dismissive, of the language other. This often means that even authors with some awareness of the language others have to omit such plurality from their accounts, and those authors who have no awareness of this do not even have to make a conscious choice as the way of writing is pregiven and pre-set.

This begs the question then to what extent academic authors are the wordsmiths of their work. In Chapter 2 I put forward the argument that 'words speak us' as a reversal of grammatical rule, but also a statement that challenges the notion of an unproblematic and pre-given authorial agency. Likewise, it could be stated that 'texts write us'. Indeed, learning how to write academic discourse and more specifically to learn to write in such a way as to be able to target particular journals have become widespread practice. Learning to write academic prose is of course hard for native speakers of English as much as for non-native speakers. Both groups attend the myriad of offers of 'writing retreats', 'boot camps', 'sweat shops' in order to develop the skill to package their ideas into (English) language that is palatable to journals in particular. A polished product of such interventions is then not so much a written text, but an academic able to produce knowledge texts that are published as peer reviewed papers (an academic genre) in journals that are ranked highly across a variety of journal ranking lists (a hierarchical structure).

In this regard the agency of authors is limited at best, as it is the product of genre and hierarchy, and authorship is suspended across these. Bringing the language other into this institutional-individual mix actually increases author agency as deliberate choices about whether and how to admit the language other into the written knowledge account need to be made. As these are not (yet) routine and automatic reporting decisions to be made, they require engagement, reflection and agentic decision making.

Regarding multilingual research, some proposals in particular in Chapters 4 and 5 were articulated about how to write about multilingual research and how to treat translation within such research projects. Overall, a comprehensive use of the term translation was proffered, to include both intralingual (i.e. meaning making in the broadest sense) and interlingual (translation between two languages) approaches. These two approaches to translation have been developed in separate parts of management literature and there are good reasons to align them. For research using interlingual translation there are additional implications for developing protocols on how to report it in written research accounts, and to develop the conceptual capacity to explore processes of institutional change within multilingual settings.

Of course, the proposals offered in Chapters 4 and 5 do not address the underlying dilemma about internalizing writing conventions and making them one's disposition. The proposals aim at offering more sophisticated ways of integrating language plurality and translation into the writing and knowledge production process. In themselves, they do not increase authorial agency as such. The only way out of this impasse is to treat translation reflexively as a means to decentre of what is taken to be 'the original' and why it is taken to be so, and the 'imitation', resulting more often than not in hybridity and perhaps even innovation. This would open up a translatorial space (Koskinen, 2020) in which knowledge is always seen as suspended and precarious.

While this book breaks a lance for languages and translation as a useful lens to unpack the research process within (multilingual) organization and the knowledge generation process itself, it is absolutely necessary to point to the limitations of this book. They relate mainly to omissions: The first limitation relates to the political aspects of organizational and management research, and while these have been discussed briefly in term of decolonization through translation, the politics of translation as a topic deserves its own book. Likewise, a second limitation takes the shape of the emphasis I have placed upon languages and translation. Of course, there are other stances and perspectives that are inscribed in our research. For example, Al Ariss, Ozbilgin, Tatli and April (2014) draw urgent attention to the ways Whiteness is inscribed into organization and management research.

Drawing on the work of Green, Sonn and Matsebula (2007) in South Africa and Australia, they identify the role of knowledge and history in reproducing the power privileges associated with Whiteness. These authors propose that the traditional rejection of research and academic investigations on the topics of history and society by non-white authors along with the indicative exclusivity of using English (or other European languages) as the language of academia is noted as an obstruction to achieving justice, and as a way of maintaining and reproducing white superiority. Likewise, gender, sexuality, religiosity and so forth are inscribed into the knowledge texts that are produced. In this regard writing from a language plurality/translation perspective restates that knowledge is not objective, but deeply embedded in history.

The final stages of this book coincide with the ongoing pandemic (COVID-19). It has uncovered 'the vulnerability of speakers who do not have access to majority languages and the growing need for translation and interpretation services around the world for public health' (Piekkari, Tietze, Angouri, Meyer & Vaara, 2021). There are unfolding agendas, which call for a new approach to the integration of languages and translation as aspects of having access to knowledge, resource and voice.

I want to finish this book with some final words about the selection of the introductory quotes as the opening pitch for each chapter. They are taken from sources near to my heart and mind, all of which I have read at least twice, all but one of which are books and their meaning and message unfold slowly over several chapters. These books are novels or biographies or some scholarly literature, and they ask questions about the relationship between words and meanings and world. They often go in circles and meaning is always shown to be malleable and changeable, as well as something that needs to be worked for: Meaning is achieved through deliberate agency, and this includes the exercise of sceptical doubt. Within these sources, experiences border on faith, the social world borders on cosmology (at times on a distorted, deeply unjust cosmos) and the notion of truth remains a possibility. Within these texts, authors are acting as enabled agents in search of meaning and truth (mainly failing). In contrast, within academic texts, authorship is necessarily more constrained as social science texts need to report and account for their respective explorations in set ways. However, whether the genre of peer-reviewed journal papers in a select group of (English language) journals remains an appropriate way forward to generate interesting, exciting and just works remains doubtful. In 1989, Richard Rorty wrote about the contingency of language and argued that – within philosophy at least – interesting ideas and cultural change do not happen because opposing ideas or their proponents engage in heated battles; rather it is more conducive to develop interesting new vocabulary that – even if half-baked – promises more innovation than repetitive battles within entrenched vocabularies. In this regard academics, who are knowledge workers and writers, need to cultivate a talent for writing differently.

It is not possible, in my slowly emergent view, and in contrast to what I have written, said and stood for in the past, to write without seeking truth while accepting that truth is not an object to be discovered. For me truth unfolds through the play of meaning as it is suspended across language and languages. In this regard the *concetto* to use non-English words and quotations, sometimes even from a language that I don't' speak, point to the delight that I found in discovering meanings that were not entailed in the English language, that were barely possible within it. In this regard putting pen to paper, as is still my wont is an act of faith that through hard work, delight, surprise and dismay, some more permanent signification can be achieved. The final words shall go to Barbara Ehrenreich, social activist, natural scientist, undercover journalist, as they raise questions of the essence of knowledge, categories and words:

> The interesting thing, some may say alarmingly, was that when you take away all human attributions – the words, the names of species, the wisps of remembered tree-related poetry, the fables of photosynthesis and the capillary action – that when you take all this away, there is still something left.
>
> (Ehrenreich, 2014, p. 48, emphasis in the original)

References

Al Ariss, A., Ozbilgin, M. F., Tatli, A. and April, K. (2014). Tackling whiteness in organization and management, *Journal of Managerial Psychology*, *29*, 4, 362–369.

Ehrenreich, B. (2014). *Living with a wild God. A non-believers search for the truth about everything.* London: Granta Books Publishing.

Green, M. J., Sonn, C. C. and Matsebula, J. (2007) Reviewing whiteness. Theory, research and possibilities, *South African Journal of Psychology*, *37*, 3, 389–419.

Höpfl, H. (2000). The suffering mother and the miserable son, organizing women and organizing women's writing. *Gender, Work and Organization*, *7*, 2, 98–105.

Koskinen, K. (2020). Translatorial linguistic ethnography in organizations. In S. Horn, P. Lecomte and S. Tietze (Eds.). *Managing the multilingual workplace: Methodological, empirical and pedagogic perspectives*, (pp. 60–78). Abingdon: Routledge.

Piekkari, R., Tietze, S., Angouri, J., Meyer, R. and Vaara, E. (2021). Can you speak Covid-19? Languages and inequality in management studies, *Journal of Management Studies*, 58, 2, 587–591.

Rorty, R. (1989). *Contingency, irony and solidarity*. Cambridge: Cambridge University Press.

Index

Űsdiken, B. 24
Usunier, J. C. 56

van Witteloostuija, A. 17
Venuti, L. 67

Welch, C. 39, 53–54
Westney, D. E. 39, 70

Westwood, R. 47–48, 49, 54
Whittle, A. 41
Wierzbicka, A. 26
Wood, M. 51

xenoglossia 19
Xian, H. 52, 55, 67

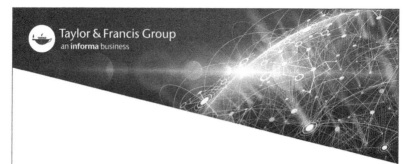